Developing an Attitude that Attracts Success

Wayne Cordeiro

DEVELOPING AN ATTITUDE THAT ATTRACTS SUCCESS

ISBN 0-9654251-8-5

First Printing November 1999.

Published by:
New Hope Resources
290 Sand Island Access Road
Honolulu, HI 96819

www.newhope-hawaii.org

Printed in the U. S. A.

Contents

Acknowledgments

I have had so many mentors over the years for whom I am eternally grateful—scores of people who have incredible spirits and attitudes of excellence. When I would observe these precious people, I would often find myself whispering, "Oh, God, make me like that too."

My earliest memories are of my mother who loved unreservedly. She stood only 4'11" tall, but she will always be a giant in my heart. A single mom, she would constantly bolster my spirit with fresh hope through her songs and her encouragement.

To my wife Anna with whom I have chosen to share my life. She has been a stable pillar of support with her gracious spirit and compassion. She has taught me so much by simply being who God made her to be.

To the many who have modeled to me the heart of God. Carol Ann Shima: you are the best encourager I have ever met. You always make people stand taller and walk more confidently after having been in your presence. Dan Shima: you are a solid fortress on the outside and a gracious servant and friend on the inside. I will always be grateful for the two of you.

I almost hesitate to start thanking those who have influenced me so much over the years because it would fill far too many pages and I fear I still might exclude more than I would remember. At least allow me to say thank you to the wonderful church of New Hope Christian Fellowship. Every single one of you has touched my life, leaving an indelible mark of the Savior's fingerprints behind.

Introduction

This book is for leaders, pastors, business people, housewives, and youth. No matter what background you are from or what your occupation may be, the principles of this book can transform your life and relationships. The only prerequisite is that you be an avid student of life.

Author Ralph Waldo Emerson once said, "The future belongs to those who prepare for it." This book will help you to do just that.

Over the years as a pastor and leader, I have watched people, studied them and observed what makes one successful and another not. I have seen talented, educated and skilled people fail. On the other hand, I have witnessed the success of those who have very little talent, education, or skill.

Many people are not that far from a life of joy and success. Just a few adjustments and life will come in loud and clear! Like a radio that's not tuned quite right, the music can be heard but it's scratchy and it vacillates in and out. It doesn't need a great deal of adjustment. A small turn of the dial will recalibrate the frequency by just a few hertz. Then all of a sudden, *Voila!* With the correct calibration, the scratchy signal is transformed into a stereophonic symphony of sound!

Your attitude is that small adjustment. It can be the difference between success and failure. Someone once said the difference between people is very small, but that very small difference is very big!

Living a life of joy and success is something God has already wired into your design! Did you know that? He preplanned your future to be one of success. In fact, God takes no joy or glory in a mediocre life. Fruitfulness is what God wants for each of us, and He's ready to help us achieve that end!

> *"You did not choose Me, but I chose you, and appointed you, that you should go and bear fruit, and that your fruit should remain, that whatever you ask of the Father in My name, He may give to you" (Jn. 15:16).*

Let God help you to develop an attitude that attracts success. He's poised to do so. Cooperate with Him. Apply the principles of this book and you'll be well on your way to fruitfulness!

My prayer for you is that you will ***live*** every day of your life!

OVERVIEW

Becoming Students of Life

I love to watch people, especially successful people; people who are successful in their families, businesses, relationships, and finances. There's a reason they're successful. Success doesn't happen by accident. People don't stumble onto it by mistake. There are solid reasons why they are successful, and they leave clues behind for us to observe and collect ... if we'll look for them. Willing students of life will be able to identify them and develop the same principles into their lives. Each of us can develop an attitude that attracts success!

"If you want to accomplish much, be much. If you want to conquer adverse circumstances, first conquer yourself. In every case, the doing must become the mere unconscious expression of the being."

—Don Polson

I remember one of my favorite pastimes while attending college in Portland, Oregon. I would go to the airport and find a nice bench adjacent to one of the thoroughfares. I would take a seat and, for an hour or two, I'd watch people.

I know what you may be thinking ... that I am a bit off-kilter. Maybe you're right, nevertheless, that's what I'd do. However, before you write me off, let me hasten to the finish.

I would see a businessman hurrying on his way to an important appointment. I would observe how he was dressed, his mannerisms, the speed with which he walked, the way he would converse with others around him, and I'd evaluate his countenance. Did he carry on his face a look of anxiety, joy, despair, or concern?

Then I would spot a young mother carrying a child from one terminal to another. I'd try to discern what kind of a person she was. Was she secure or fearful? What kind of day was she having? Was she successful? Was there peace in her heart or worry?

I'd watch students, workers, airport officials and others as they walked to and fro in the concourse. I'd observe the way they would stand, sit, walk, and communicate with one another or the focus of their eyes when in conversation. I would observe them as they walked by, watching their conversation, how they would greet the friend or family member who came to pick them up. In every case, I would ponder what it was that made one person successful and another not. What made one life happier and more joy-filled, while another would be empty and hollow?

"Outstanding people have one thing in common: an absolute sense of mission."

—ZIG ZIGLAR

Each of their lives had a story behind them ... a story of struggle or success, of abandon or hope, of pessimism or promise.

Over the years, I've collected and catalogued scores of observations of failure and success. I've attempted to distill these principles of life and record them for students of life.

Never stop learning. Make it a lifelong goal. Discovering new truths and insights will awaken your spirit, and new horizons will help you to always look ahead and focus on your potential rather than your problems, your future rather than your failures.

The Fellowship of the White Belt

I remember reading about the founder of the martial art of judo: Jigoro Kano. Jigoro Kano was the highest-ranking black belt of his time, a man greatly respected in worldwide circles. Kano possessed an extraordinary willingness to learn. He sought out the then nearly defunct martial art of jujitsu and modified it to incorporate modern sports principles, creating the revised martial art of judo.

Kano was so focused on learning improved techniques that he found new and better ways for the island nation of Japan to educate, and was soon given the honorary title of "the father of modern Japanese education." Kano became world-famous and well respected in many social and political arenas.

And what about judo, the sport he founded? It became the defense system of the Japanese police and was added as the first eastern martial art in international competition at the Olympics. His story is a lesson of inspiration and motivation for every student of life.

Just before he died, this world-renowned martial arts expert called his students together. As they congregated to hear the final words of their judo master, he announced, "When you bury me, do not bury me in a black belt! Be sure to bury me in a white belt!"

In martial arts the white belt is a symbol of a beginner, an apprentice realizing he or she has many things yet to learn.

What a lesson in humility and teachability! Each of us, regardless of our ranking in life, must be lifelong learners and students. Whether you are a CEO, a pastor, leader, elder, or teacher, under all your roles, always wear a white belt. Even if you are an expert in your field, continue to value learning. By continuing to learn you will continue to be an expert. As soon as we stop learning, we begin to stiffen up and atrophy!

"Each of us, regardless of our ranking in life, must be lifelong learners and students."

—Wayne Cordeiro

Profiles of Two Heroes

People often ask me who my heroes are. One is Wendy Stoker. Wendy attended a Midwest high school, and in her final year finished just 3.5 points behind first place in girl's diving. She went on to complete her education at an East Coast college. There she took a full load of classes, she was on the bowling team, involved herself in student government, and of course continued her diving. But what was most spectacular about this young college freshman was her typing skills. She typed at a "whizzing" ... well, sort of ... 40 words per minute.

I forgot to mention that Wendy Stoker was born without arms. She types 40 words per minute with her toes.

"I have not failed 10,000 times. I have successfully found 10,000 ways that will not work."

—Thomas Edison *(after trying an experiment 10,000 times).*

What is it that causes such determination, such courage, and such indomitable spirit? Before I discuss that, let me share with you another of my heroes who is none other than Thomas Alva Edison: the inventor of the incandescent light bulb, the movie film, and the batteries we use to start our cars.

Toward the autumn years of his life, he kept his work housed in an old wooden structure that resembled a barn. There with his son, Edison would often be found late into the night laboring to perfect his inventions.

One evening, in an experiment to improve the retention of the battery's charge, there was a miscombination of chemicals. Within minutes, the heat generated caused a chemical combustion. It wasn't long before the wooden frame caught fire, and what began as a small flame exploded into a towering inferno. Fire engulfed the structure as Thomas Edison's son evacuated the building. Using his smock as a shroud, he desperately called back for his father fearing he may choose to remain in the barn only to perish along with his precious life's work.

Running frantically, he circled the barn hoping his father may have exited by another opening. Protecting his eyes from the intense heat, he continued calling for his father. On his second time around the building he turned the corner and to his glad relief, there stood his legendary father. His hands were buried deep in his soot-speckled smock, his white hair blackened with ash. He was watching intently as the flames devoured the structure.

"Father!" cried Edison's son. "I was so afraid you'd still be inside!"

"If we did all the things we are capable of, we would literally astound ourselves."

—Thomas Edison

Without taking his eyes off the flames, Thomas Edison, with a sense of urgency, said, "Son, go get your mother!"

"Why, Dad?" he replied.

With a twinkle in his eyes his father replied, "Because your mother comes from a small town and she's never seen a fire like this one before!"

And when the flames had finished their work, leaving only the leftovers of ash and twisted frame, Edison turned to his son.

"In heroes well known or unsung, you'll find one common thread, one common denominator. In every case, it is attitude! That's right. Your attitude is more important than you will ever realize."

—Wayne Cordeiro

"You know anyone who has a tractor?"

"Yes, dad, but why?"

Thomas Edison answered, "Because it's time to rebuild, boy. It's time to rebuild."

Both Wendy Stoker and Thomas Edison ... what great models for each of us! But what is it that kept them going though the odds were stacked against them? What was the fuel that compelled them beyond their setbacks?

In heroes well known or unsung, you'll find one common thread, one common denominator. In every case, it is attitude! That's right. Your attitude is more important than you will ever realize.

Your attitude is the most important thing about you. It is more important than your education, more important than your past, more important than your looks, more important than your money, more important than ***anything.*** Your attitude will either help you make friends or make enemies. It will attract people to you or repel people from you. Your attitude is even more important than your skills. John D. Rockefeller once said, "I will pay a man more for his attitude and his ability to get along with others than for any other skill he may possess." Your attitude is one of your most important assets.

"people who are effective have used ... setbacks as steppingstones, whereas ineffective people have used them as excuses."

—Wayne Cordeiro

It's not necessarily the current state of your family, your problems, who your boss is or how much money you make. It will be your attitude *towards* family, *towards* problems, *towards* authority, and *towards* money that makes all the difference in the world!

You'll find both effective and ineffective people have the same amount of setbacks. However, the people who are effective have used those setbacks as steppingstones, whereas ineffective people have used them as excuses.

"A happy person is not a person in a certain set of circumstances, but rather a person with a certain set of attitudes."

—Hugh Downs

I am absolutely convinced of the truth behind the maxim, "Life is made up of 10 percent what happens to you and 90 percent how you *respond* to what happens to you." That's where character is built. That's where personality is formed. That's where attitude is expressed.

You can have two people: both from the same schools, had the same teachers, shop at the same stores, live in the same city, and even attend the same church. One struggles and the other is successful. Why?

Attitude.

A Fragrance or An Odor: The Choice is Yours

In Hawaii, we have a custom of giving *leis* to one another as an act of hospitality, honor, or friendship. A *lei* is usually made up of flowers strung together and hung around a person's neck. We give *leis* to say, "Thank you" and we give *leis* to say, "Goodbye."

I love the fragrant flowers of Hawaii. The *pikake*, *plumeria*, white ginger and the *pua kenikeni* are among my favorites. The smell of these beautiful flowers are so pungent that everywhere I turn, the wafting fragrance adds a sense of Polynesian *aloha* to everything I experience.

When I have one of these *leis* on, regardless of whom I meet, they all smell wonderful! They may be tall or short, happy or sad, coming with a complaint or a compliment, yet they all smell wonderful to me! And this fragrance has nothing to do with them. It has everything to do with the *lei* I have on! Isn't that great!

Our attitude is like a *lei*. Each of us has one, but we have the choice of what we are going to string together to make up that *lei*. If you string together a collection of dried fish, everything starts to smell fishy! If you string together old socks, the whole world has this funny odor to it. Your attitude is like a fragrance you carry around with you. The difference is that skunks carry around an ***odor*** while a beautiful, Hawaiian *plumeria* blossom carries a ***fragrance***. Whether you like it or not, each of us carries one of the above. You choose which it will be. Some people's poor attitude follows them around like bad cologne. Others who have wonderful personalities leave a fragrance in their wake as they pass through our lives.

"My life is my message."
—Mahatma Gandhi

Attitudes Affect Our Health

Your attitude will even affect your physical health. When there is the presence of stress or worry, your body secretes a powerful hormone from your adrenal glands called *adrenaline*. The effects of adrenaline in our bodies can be compared to rocket fuel in a missile or nitric oxide in a racecar. It shoots nuclear fuel into your veins in the presence of danger. It is designed to give you an immediate boost of energy or strength.

When I was jogging some time ago, I passed by a fenced yard that was the domain of two massive Dobermans. I didn't see these dogs ("flesh-eating canines" would be a better term) as I jogged past the yard. I guess they felt I was jogging too close to their boundary line, so out of nowhere, they bolted towards the fence. At the time of the attack, I didn't realize there was anything separating their ugly teeth from my pristine body. All I heard were these loud, vicious, blood-curdling barks, and from the corner of my eye I saw two demonic figures fiercely charging towards me.

Adrenaline shot through my body like a bullet through soft cheese. I jumped three or four feet straight into the air and darted off faster than I had ever run since high school.

Adrenaline is a powerful chemical designed to be burned up immediately. However, if it is not, it can affect you adversely. Your body doesn't know if it is being attacked from the inside or from the outside. Having a critical attitude puts your body on an "all points alert" system. It goes on the defensive. If I carry around with me a bad attitude, small doses of adrenaline drip into my blood stream, all day long. With the presence of adrenaline in our system, we get irritable, we are cynical, we get old faster, we hurt, and even though we go to bed at night, we are still tired when we awake.

Doctors say that stress and worry cause more internal damage than we realize. Physiologically, we are affected by fears, insecurity, and unresolved bitterness. It weakens our immune system, which causes us to become susceptible to viruses and diseases we would have normally been resistant towards.

A dear friend of mine was the picture of health. He ate only the best foods, exercised, and watched his cholesterol levels vigilantly. But he had one major malady: worry. He worried about whatever he could not control until it ate him up on the inside. He had a tough time trusting God for his future, his finances, or his family. He'd constantly have stomach ailments from stress and fears. I observed that as his anxiety grew, so did his age. He seemed to be in his sixties even though he was only 52. The handwriting seemed to be emblazoned across the wall as I watched him go through his second divorce. The telltale signs of too much stress had cost him another loving relationship.

This dear friend recently passed away at an early age. Although a health nut, he had succumbed to something much more devastating: a terrible perspective on life.

It was this attitude that stole his best years.

Did you know that the presence of adrenaline in your blood system can increase your cholesterol count 40 percent! Often we go on these exotic diets and take pills to reduce our cholesterol level when what will reduce it more effectively is a better attitude toward life!

I guess you can say your health is determined not so much by what you're eating, but more by *what's eating you!*

"Hardening of the attitudes is the most deadly disease on the face of this earth."

—Zig Ziglar

Your Attitude Affects Everything about You

A man made an appointment to see his doctor. "Doctor," he pleaded, "everywhere I touch seems to hurt lately. Am I getting old or just senile? If I push here on my knees, why, my knees ache. I push on my stomach and my stomach hurts! I press on my head here by my right temple, and that hurts too! What's going on?"

"I guess you can say that your health is determined not so much by what you're eating, but more by what's eating you!"

—Wayne Cordeiro

The doctor quickly saw that this man must be having abnormal problems and called for a full body x-ray.

An hour passed and after evaluating the x-rays carefully, the doctor returned. Stroking his chin, the doctor slowly began, "I think I've found the reason why everything you touch, hurts."

"Well, tell me!" the man anxiously replied.

The doctor pointed to the x-ray, "Your body is fine, but it's your finger. It's broken."

Our attitude is like that finger. If our attitude stinks, everything stinks. If our attitude is good, everything is fragrant!

How's your attitude? Is it more like an odor that follows you around? Or is it a beautiful fragrance that makes any situation more pleasant? Take some time right now to evaluate yourself.

CHAPTER ONE

Your Attitude is a Choice

"Blessed are the poor in spirit, for theirs is the kingdom of heaven. Blessed are the gentle, for they shall inherit the earth. Blessed are the merciful, for they shall receive mercy. Blessed are the pure in heart, for they shall see God. Blessed are the peacemakers, for they shall be called sons of God" (Matthew 5:3, 5, 7-9).

"Successful people go to the Word of God, learn what is right, and do it."
—DALE GALLOWAY

Jesus' very first teaching to His disciples addressed their attitudes (Matthew 5:3-12). Theologians have termed it the "Beatitudes." I guess it could be said, *"your attitudes will determine what you will be,"* hence the *be-attitudes.*

He knew that developing a correct perspective on life was critically important to their lives and to their ministries, and so He themed His very first discourse on that very topic. In fact, before Jesus taught His disciples about miracles, discipleship, or how to deal with the Pharisees, He taught them about attitudes! Every phrase deals with building right attitudes because they become the *"lamp of our bodies,"* (Mt. 6:22-23) the very way we see events and interpret them.

Why?

"That which we are, we are all the while teaching, not voluntarily but involuntarily."

—Ralph Waldo Emerson

An interesting scientific theorem states: "If your basic premise is inaccurate, then every subsequent conclusion thereafter will also be inaccurate." What this means is that if you are solving math problems and you begin with 2 + 2 = 5, then all of your following calculations will be incorrect. If my core attitudes and perspectives toward life and people are skewed, then I too will experience massacre after massacre in relationships, foiled expectations, and broken dreams.

Jesus knew that from the core of our beings, we need to develop a right attitude towards life. This is why He said, *"The lamp of the body is the eye."* (Mt. 6:22-23). Let the "eye" of your attitude be clear and your every conclusion thereafter will result in success after success!

Poor Attitudes Cost

The president of the Bank of America told this story which took place some years ago:

The Los Angeles branch of the Bank of America is housed in a multi-level building with a parking structure on its lower floors. This large skyscraper housed many businesses. For many years, customers using the bank would not be charged for parking if they simply presented a ticket to the teller for validation with any transaction.

Over the years, however, people slowly began abusing this privilege by making small or insignificant transactions at the bank, then spend the rest of the day shopping at the other businesses housed in the same building. Due to the consistent infractions by shrewd customers, the bank reluctantly discontinued the privilege of validating tickets for free and unlimited parking. Every validation now required, although discounted, a small cost per hour that each customer would pay.

"Remember not only to say the right thing in the right place, but far more difficult still, to leave unsaid the wrong thing at the tempting moment."

—Benjamin Franklin

One morning, an elderly man dressed in jeans and a flannel shirt waited his turn in the line of customers. The line slowly inched its way forward until he made his way to the next open teller's booth. He made a small deposit, and then presented his ticket for validation. The teller stamped his ticket and informed him that he would have to pay a small amount for the parking.

"Why, you've never required this before," he replied.

The teller, facing a crowded bank fueled by long lines of impatient customers, snapped, "Well that's the new rule. I don't make 'em. I just dish 'em out."

"But I've been a customer in this bank for many years," he persisted. "The least you can do is validate it like you used to."

"Act as if what you do makes a difference. It does."

—William James

"You heard me, Mister. You got a problem with that, see the manager. I have a lot of people waiting behind you. If you could move along, that would make this morning go by a little easier."

The flannel-shirted gentleman made his way to the end of the long line of waiting customers and once again inched his way back towards the tellers' booths. When he finally arrived, he approached the first available teller, withdrew 4.2 million dollars, and went across the street to another bank and deposited it there.

That was an attitude that cost the bank 4.2 million dollars! Never underestimate the destruction of a poor attitude!

A sign hanging on the wall of an old gas station holds for us a poignant truth. It reads:

Why Customers Quit

1% die. 3% move. 5% quit because of location. 7% quit because of product dissatisfaction. But 84% of customers quit because of an attitude of indifference shown to them by one of the employees!

Choose Life!

"I call heaven and earth to witness against you today, that I have set before you life and death, the blessing and the curse. So choose life in order that you may live." (Deut. 30:19).

God tells us that the choice between life and death, a blessing or a curse is up to us! He almost pleads with His followers telling them to "*choose life in order that you may live!*" God not only gives us the choice, He goes further to tell us what choice to make. He even lets us know the consequences if we refuse to make that choice as well as the benefits of making the right choice!

"Unhappiness is in not knowing what we want & killing ourselves to get it."

—Don Herold

In essence, here's what God is saying: "Here's your choice, life or death, a fruitful future or one of pain. But wait! Before you choose, let Me tell you which is best. Choose life that you may live, both you and your descendants. Got it? Okay, now choose."

God Even Shows Us the Way

How many of you remember "Let's Make a Deal"? I remember this early 1970s television game show because the people would dress up like chickens, ducks, and hogs, and then act nuts. Monty Hall, the show's host, would say, "Chicken, come on down!" A lady dressed like a chicken would run down. There were three doors and he would say, "Okay! Choose door one, two, or three! Which one are you going to choose?" The crowd would yell out, "One!" "No pick two!" "Three! Three! Pick three!" all at the same time.

She'd choose, "Three!"

He'd say, "Before I show you what's behind door number three, let me show you what's behind door number one!" He'd open it up and there would be five Mercedes Benz deluxe automobiles.

Wails of sorrow would rise from the chicken as well as from the audience. Monty would continue, "Now let me show you what's behind door number two!" The door swings open and a voice announces, "A free vacation in Acapulco!"

I press on toward the goal to win the prize for which God has called me heavenward in Christ Jesus.

(PHILIP. 3:14)

More groans of disappointment.

"And now," continued the announcer, "let me show you what's behind door number three! This is what you chose!" He'd open the door and it would be a donkey.

The chicken lady was so upset she would throw her hands up in despair as the audience echoed her woe for such a poor choice.

Isn't that tragic? But do you want to know what would be even more tragic? If it would have been like this:

"What door will you choose? Door one, two, or three? But wait! Before you choose, let me *show you* what's behind every door! Door number one, five Mercedes Benz deluxe automobiles! Door number two, a free vacation in Acapulco! Door number three, a dumb donkey! Got it?"

"Uh, okay!" the chicken lady replies, and the crowd goes wild in anticipation.

"Now, which one will you choose? Door number one, door number two, or door number three?"

She pauses for a second amidst the confusing barnyard calls of the other animals in the studio audience.

"Oh... Uh... Well..." she nervously deliberates her final decision. "Door number three!"

Now *that* would be tragic!

Nevertheless, as dumb as that sounds, that's exactly what we do. How often has God shown us the consequences of a bad choice or walking through life with a bad attitude, and yet we choose that attitude anyway. Then when relationships fail, when we lose friends or forfeit a great opportunity, it's really no surprise.

> *"Have this attitude in you which was also in Christ Jesus" (Philip. 2:5).*

Take the time with me over these next chapters to deposit into your heart the necessary ingredients to develop a life-changing attitude. Make that choice right now. It may come slowly at first, but don't give up. It may even feel awkward, but practice until it becomes natural.

"You are only one attitude away from a great life, a successful marriage, and a promising future!"
—Wayne Cordeiro

You are only one attitude away from a great life, a successful marriage, and a promising future!

CHAPTER TWO

Believe that You Can Change

"You will be ruled by the rudder or you will be ruled by the rocks. The choice is yours."

We ... are being transformed into his likeness with ever-increasing glory, which comes from the Lord, who is the Spirit.

(2 Cor. 3:18)

No one has been given an unalterable attitude. You can change, but it's up to you. Decide now what kind of attitude you want to approach life with and develop it. However, that doesn't mean it will simply happen. You must develop it, and the sooner you begin the better.

Some people hide behind the excuse that they just can't change. "I've been this way since I was a kid, and I'm not about to change now!"

It's never too late to change! Change is irreducible to growth. If you stop changing, you stop growing, and if you stop growing, you're in trouble! What do you call a tree that has stopped growing? That's right. *Dead!* And it's no different with people. When they stop growing, they start dying. In fact, some people stopped growing years ago. Family members might not bury them till they've *stopped moving,* but they've really died years before! You *can* change your attitude.

Thank goodness for one church secretary who was willing to change her attitude. One Monday morning, a tall Texan wearing a ten gallon hat sauntered into the church office and saddled up to the counter.

"I came in to talk with the head pig of this here church," he confidently drawled with a heavy southern accent.

"The head ... what!?" the secretary replied with obvious shock in her voice.

"Life is change. Growth is optional. Choose wisely."

—Karen Kaiser Clark

"The head pig. Ya' know, the one who blabs on and on every Sunday morning. Just wanted to talk with him before I head back to the ranch," the Texan continued, drawing out each syllable along the way.

Aghast at his irreverence, the prim-and-proper secretary straightened herself in her chair. With a voice that resembled a reprimanding grade school teacher, she retorted: "Now listen here. We don't use such terms of disrespect in this office! We might call him 'Reverend' or 'Pastor,' but never anything less!"

"Well," he drawled, "I never meant no disrespect, ma'am. I just sold a bunch of my stock and heard the good Lord tell me to donate a million dollars. Thought I'd like to do that here."

With a new sparkle in her voice she quickly responded,

"Wait right there. I'll go get the hog!" You must be quick to change!

A famous inventor said, "The world hates change, yet it is the only thing that has brought progress."

How open are you to change? There can be no growth without change. When we refuse to change and resist God's leading, He can make it pretty miserable! You see, sometimes we won't change until the pain of remaining the same becomes greater than the pain of changing.

What Will Navigate Your Life?

Before technology changed the way we navigate ships, bullhorns and whistles were used to communicate from ship to ship. It was in a shrouded, fogged-in bay, when a large armored battleship was slowly making its way through uncharted waters.

Suddenly through the fog, the captain noticed what seemed to be the light of another ship directly in his path. Quickly, through the megaphone he shouted, "This is Admiral Smith of the United States Navy. Steer yourself ten degrees south. We are on a collision course, and I am coming through with priority orders."

"When you're finished changing, you're finished."

—Benjamin Franklin

Through the fog, he heard a faint but audible reply, "This is Seaman Fourth Class Jones. You steer yourself ten degrees to the north."

The Admiral said to himself, "He is a seaman fourth class, and I'm an admiral! Who in the world does he think he is?"

Turning up the megaphone a few notches and using a stronger tone of authority, he barked back, "This is Admiral Smith of the United States Navy! You steer your vessel ten degrees south! I'm coming through!"

Through the fog, the unrelenting reply repeated, "This is Seaman Fourth Class Jones. You steer yourself ten degrees north."

The admiral's anger flared at such insubordination. "I said this is Admiral Smith of the U.S. Navy. You steer yourself ten degrees south! I am a battleship!"

Through the fog, the unwavering insubordinate replied, "This is Seaman Fourth Class Jones. You steer yourself ten degrees north. *I am a lighthouse!*"

Our attitudes are like the rudder of a ship. You will either be ruled by the rudder or you will be ruled by the rocks.

The choice is yours.

An Issue of Faith

As is thy faith, so shall it be done unto thee.

(Mt. 9:29)

If we refuse to change, we're in trouble! If you think you can't change, you won't have the faith to change even if it becomes available. The Bible says, *"As is thy faith, so shall it be done unto thee"* (Mt. 9:29). If I don't have the faith that I can change or that my situation can change, then it won't. On the other hand, if I say: "I can change; I can clean up; I can follow Jesus; I can be a man devoted; God can use me; my marriage can change," then the Lord can say: "Now you've got the faith." It releases the Lord to do His work. If I say I can't, then I won't have the faith to cooperate with God's attempts to bring wholeness and healing. I will actually sabotage God's work in me.

Do you believe your marriage can change? You must believe it can. You must be able to believe that your heart can change, that your family situation can change. God is able. The question is, "Are you willing?"

Often in the Bible, God commends or reprimands people based on the level of their faith. In Luke 8, a woman who had been ill for over 12 years heard that Jesus was passing through. She honestly believed she would be healed if she could only *"touch the fringe of His cloak."* When she did, Jesus answered and said, *"Your faith has made you well!"*

"God is able. The question is, 'Are you willing?'"

—Wayne Cordeiro

How much faith do you have that you can change? You must believe you can be made well, that you can develop an attitude that attracts success. If you don't think you can, you won't. The choice is up to you.

No One Told Him It Couldn't Be Done

His name was George Dansig. Everybody knew that in this southern California college, whoever achieved the best grade on the upcoming final exam would be offered the

"It's not who you are that holds you back, it's who you think you're not."

—Bob Moawad

one and only position as the next assistant math professor.

George wanted it so badly he couldn't sleep at night. His lifelong dream was to become a math professor, and this was his golden opportunity! Nothing must stand in his way. He had to get all the answers correct. He became obsessed with his dream. On the day of the final, he found himself studying so intently that when he looked at his watch, he discovered he was already 15 minutes late for the test! Pangs of anxiety gripped him as he knew he'd have to make up the time lost.

He quickly collected his books, ran down the hallway, and slid into the room. Attempting to apologize for his tardiness, the professor whispered, *"Shhh,"* gave him a ream of papers containing the test, and motioned for him to get started.

The test was more difficult than he expected, but his drive motivated him on until he completed all the questions. However, just as he was about to turn his test in, he noticed the professor had posted two more problems on the chalkboard. Figuring these for extra credit, he turned his paper over, and began.

An excruciating battle of mind over math began, but his efforts would not be in vain. The invisible guardian over the science of math seemed to recognize his efforts and rewarded him with the answer to the first query. And now for the second problem.

He began with the zeal of a trained athlete, but soon knew he had met his match. Beads of sweat began to form on his brow. George knew that if he didn't solve this one last problem, someone else would! He would then be denied the one and only position of his dreams. Just then, the professor said, "Time's up!"

George pleaded, "Oh, professor! Five more minutes!"

He said, "I'm sorry, George. We must be fair. Turn in your test."

Dejected, knowing someone else was going to get all of them correct, George slumped back like a defeated contestant. That night he couldn't sleep, he tossed and turned. The next morning, he almost had to force himself to come back to class. His greatest fear was knowing he would hear someone else's name mentioned as the new assistant math professor.

He slowly entered the room, but when he did, the professor stood up behind his desk and said, "Mr. George Dansig! You have made mathematical history!"

George said, "I don't understand, sir."

The professor replied, "Oh, you were late yesterday, weren't you, George?"

"Yes, sir. I'm sorry. I was studying."

"No, no! Let me explain," he continued. "You see, George, this was going to be a hard test. So I warned the students before the final began that there are some very, very difficult problems in mathematics and this would be no exception. In fact, there are some problems so difficult they are called 'unsolvable math problems.' As an example, I wrote two of them on the board, and you solved one of them!"

Let me ask you this question: If George was told he couldn't solve the problem, that it was impossible, do you think he would have even tried? Absolutely not!

Believe that you can change and you will.

You Gotta Believe!

One man says, "I can," and another says, "I cannot." Which one is correct?

Both.

The Bible says, *"As a man thinketh, so is he"* (Pr. 23:7). Jesus comments to the blind men in Matthew 9:29, *"Be it done to you according to your faith."*

The story is told about a Scotsman whose work ethic characterized him as an extremely hard worker. He not only held himself to a high standard but set the same for those who were under him. During one project where he was setting seemingly impossible deadlines for his men, a coworker teased him saying, "Hey Scotty! Don't you know that Rome wasn't built in a day?"

"Yes, I read about that," he replied. "That's because I wasn't the foreman on that job!"

"Argue for your limitations, and sure enough, they're yours."
—Richard Bach

Do you accept the normal limitations that stop everyone else? Are you willing to accept what others accept? Don't do it! That will be the beginning of mediocrity.

Remember the bumblebee. According to the theory of aerodynamics, it should be scientifically impossible for the bumblebee to fly. Its size, weight, and shape of its body in relation to its wingspread make it theoretically impossible for flight. But no one told the bumblebee, so it flies anyway, whatever scientists might say!

Jeremiah 29:11 says, *"'For I know the plans that I have for you,' declares the Lord, 'plans for welfare and not for calamity to give you a future and a hope.'"*

If God has great plans for our lives, isn't it time we believe the same? Isn't it time we believe what God believes? That's called faith and your attitude level reflects your faith level! That's why your attitude is so critical. It is the barometer of your faith.

When the great architect Frank Lloyd Wright was 83 years old, he was asked which of his works would be his greatest masterpiece. He replied, "My next one!"

The future is brighter when your attitude is right. You'll have more energy, your creativity level will increase, and you'll stay younger!

Where's the Storm?

"The smallest of boats are safe in the roughest of seas, just so long as none of that rough sea gets inside that small boat!"

Developing an attitude that attracts success is an inside job. You see, having a godly attitude does not mean the absence of problems or storms.

But Jesus answered, "O you men of little faith! Why are you so frightened?" Then he stood up and rebuked the wind and waves, and the storm subsided and all was calm.

(Mt. 8:26)

I can't remember where I heard it, but an old poem I came across went something like this:

One ship sails East
and another sails West,
While the selfsame
breezes blow.
But it's the set of the sail
and not the winds
That determines
where it will go.
And as the storms rage on
as we journey through life,
It will be the set of our hearts
that determines where we go,
Not the storms or strife.

Your attitude is like the set of your sail. You must choose the direction you want your life to travel and set your heart towards it. Indeed there will be storms, but it will be your attitude towards those storms that will drive you in one direction or another, not the storm itself.

Each of us will be surrounded with problems and often find ourselves steeped in hot water. But remember that the event itself will soon pass. The event is temporary, but how we respond in the midst of the event will last much longer. For some, poor attitudes in the midst of the storm can cause the storm to rage on for a lifetime. It is our attitudes that turn an outside storm into an inside storm.

Never Let Outside Storms Become Inside Storms

We will always have storms in our lives, but always remember to never allow an outside storm to become an inside storm.

It's these inside storms that sink ships.

The Bible is replete with story after story of how God's people encountered problems.

When Noah sailed the ocean blue,
He had problems the same as you.
For forty days he drove the ark,
Before he found a place to park.

How many times have we found ourselves flooded with problems? Often when I have been surrounded with struggles in the ministry, I have felt like the lion tamer who put an ad in the paper:

"Lion tamer—Wants tamer lion."

A few years ago, I took up the hobby of fishing with some friends off the eastern shore of the Big Island of Hawaii. We would throw our lines into the ocean and if we were fishing at the right time and had the right bait, we'd catch some fair-sized fish!

Nearby was a barbecue grill where we would prepare the fish for dinner. We would take our day's catch, clean each one, and then place each trophy on the grill.

Even though these fish lived all of their lives (albeit brief) in the salty ocean, guess what I had to sprinkle on the fish as we were cooking them? Right! I'd sprinkle some salt on the meat to bring out the flavor.

You would think that would be about the most unnecessary thing to do since the fish had been marinating itself in saltwater for a year or two.

How interesting! Even though these fish lived in the ocean, none of the salt got on the inside of it to flavor its meat. Now if God can do that for fish, He can do that for each of us.

Each of us has been placed in the middle of a world filled with worldly perspectives and philosophies. However, here's the wonder of God's design! Although we live in the midst of a "crooked and perverse generation," none of that "crooked and perverseness" is supposed to get inside of us!

Your attitude will either protect you or defeat you in the midst of the storms. Develop your attitude well.

See Negatives as Changing

A few people have said to me, "I understand what you're saying about looking for what's right. But you can't deny that there are problems! There *will always* be problems, and they *do* exist. How do you deal with them, practically?"

"Whenever you speak of problems, always speak of them as changing."
—Wayne Cordeiro

Sure there will be problems and each problem needs to be addressed. You need to meet them head on and courageously deal with them in a way that honors God and builds biblical character. However, here's a secret that has helped me over the years: whenever you speak of problems, always speak of them as *changing*.

Someone says, "You have a problem." Your response should be, "Yes, I do, but it's *changing!*" Someone else says, "Well, you've got financial problems." Your answer? "Yes, but that's *changing!*" When someone says to you, "Hey, you have a bad marriage." You get to say, "Yeah, but it's *changing!*" When someone says "You've got bad breath!" you can reply, "Yeah, but it's *changing!*"

When you speak of problems as changing, it gives you a hopeful light at the end of the darkened tunnel. This is a positive indicator that you are in the process of growing. However, if someone says, "You've got financial problems" and you say, "Man, do I ever have financial problems! I have always HAD financial problems and I'll always HAVE financial problems. Until Jesus comes, I will have financial problems!" This attitude acts as a magnet and invites depression and cynicism. It shuts down your creative problem solving and causes you to "freeze up" in the state you are in.

You will see problems everywhere but don't allow your eyes to remain focused on them. Look for the answers and that's what you will see. Develop a new perspective and a fresh view of your problems. Solve them. Don't dwell on them. You'll be tempted to remain in a slough of despair. It feels good, sometimes, to be pitied and find increasing reasons to remain polarized. But don't do it. Failure is not when you get knocked down. Failure is when you refuse to get back up. Don't hang around the swamps of despair. It will only serve to skew your attitude and impede your resilience. Learn to bounce back quickly.

"For the righteous man falls seven times, and rises again..."

(Proverbs 24:16)

Someone once said to me, *"When you go through hell, don't stop to take pictures."*

I agree!

CHAPTER THREE

Train Your Eyes to See What is Good

"He who diligently seeks good seeks favor, but he who searches after evil, it will come to him." (Proverbs 11:27)

All our life, we've trained our eyes to see what is bad.

From our earliest recollection, we have been training ourselves incorrectly. We get up and read the local morning newspaper, which is filled with bad news. If that wasn't enough to fill our reservoir, we stop by a newsstand and buy the *U.S. Bad News and World Report* so we can find out what's bad in the world. We rush home from work, watch the 5 o'clock bad news, and stay up late to watch it all over again on the ten o'clock bad news. We are then prepared to have a bad sleep with bad dreams, only to get up with a bad attitude so we can have another bad day at work. And we've done that every day for years!

We have to retrain our eyes. The reason is this: Whatever we're looking for, is what we will see! That's just how God made us. If we are looking for good, we will see what's good. If we're always looking for what's wrong with people, guess what we'll see everywhere we turn? We will see what's wrong. But if we look for what's right with people, then we'll see the most beautiful people in the world everywhere we turn.

The lamp of the body is the eye; if therefore your eye is clear, your whole body will be full of light. But if your eye is bad, your whole body will be full of darkness. If therefore the light that is in you is darkness, how great is the darkness!

(MT. 6:22-23)

In 1984, when we moved to a quiet little town called Hilo on the southernmost island in the Hawaiian chain of islands, my wife came home one day and announced, "Honey! I know what I want!"

"What?" I asked.

"I want a Mazda MPV van. Buy me one!" she pleaded.

"Uh huh..." I grunted.

She said, "It's a beautiful van!"

I had never seen a Mazda van. Up to this time, all I had seen were Mazda passenger cars. "Mazda doesn't make vans. I've never seen one."

She said, "Oh, yes! They make them! They're beautiful vans! That's what I want!"

"Honey, Mazda doesn't make vans."

She said, "Yes they do! Jump in the car!"

We climbed into the car and took a trek into town. Within 15 minutes, a Mazda van pulled through an intersection we were approaching. My wife exclaimed, "There's one!"

I said, "That *is* nice! I didn't realize Mazda made vans."

Within 15 minutes, another one came by. She said, "There's another one! And that's the color I want! If you love me..."

Within the hour, we had seen six Mazda vans! I didn't even think they had been manufactured the week before, but now they were everywhere! Isn't that true? If you're thinking of purchasing a certain car, you notice them everywhere! Everyone's driving that car!

What you're looking for, you begin to see.

Look for Evidence of His Presence

Train your eyes to see evidence of God's presence, not evidence of His absence. If you are looking for God's absence, you'll conclude that this world is a God-forsaken place! On the other hand, if you are looking for evidence of His presence, you'll be able to see that He is with us even in the darkest of moments.

"Train your eyes to see evidence of God's presence, not evidence of His absence."

—Wayne Cordeiro

Sometimes we have a mistaken definition of "spirituality." This malady can infect all Christians without favoritism, but it more often strikes older Christians who have been in churches for five years or more. These seem to be the most prone and susceptible. When stricken by this disease, once stalwart Christians are now pharisaical at best. One telltale sign heralding the presence of this disease is when we begin to think that spiritual maturity is measured by how many faults we can detect in others. If I can see more faults than anyone else, then obviously I'm more spiritually mature.

If you are looking for cursing, curses will find you! If you are not looking for what's good, then even what good there is present will be difficult to recognize!

> *"He loved cursing, so it came to him, and he did not delight in blessings, so they were far from him" (Ps. 109:17).*

Change the Definition

One way to give you staying power is to change your definition of the event. For the way in which you define something will determine, to a large degree, how you will respond to that event.

"...the way in which you define something will determine, to a large degree, how you will respond to that event."

—Wayne Cordeiro

I lived in Eugene, Oregon for many years. Eugene is known for, among other things, its gray skies and rain. Being from Hawaii, the absence of the sun's warm rays on my body took a toll on me each winter. Believe it or not, I actually resorted to buying a sun lamp one year when I felt I was about to die from a lack of sun exposure!

I remember walking to a coffee shop, one November morning with a friend, when it began to rain. Not looking forward to another rainy day, I complained, "*Phooey!* Rain again! I wish it would quit!"

My friend's response surprised me. *"Hooray!"* he cheered exuberantly. "Rain! I love it!"

"What in the world are you celebrating this horrible weather for?" I rebuked.

"Because this tells me it's snowing on the mountains! Ski season has begun!"

My friend was an avid skier. He had defined "rain" as the early beginnings of a great ski season. I, on the other hand, had defined it as another day of depression and sun lamp therapy at home.

Between each event and your attitude toward that event lies your *definition* of that event.

> *"Consider [define] it as all joy my brethren when you encounter various trials..." (James 1:2).*

"Between each event and your attitude toward that event lies your definition of that event."

—Wayne Cordeiro

James instructs us to define our events carefully because it will affect our attitudes and actions. In fact, not only does he tell us to define them carefully, he tells us to define it all as *joy*. Not just some, not just the good times, but *all* of our circumstances, including trials, are to be defined as *joy*.

How can we possibly do that? Read as James continues:

> *"...knowing that the testing of your faith produces endurance and let endurance have its perfect result that you may be perfect*

and complete lacking nothing" (James 1:3-4).

We get to define it *all* as *joy*, even the trials, when we know the positive outcome it can have on our lives—in deepening our faith, in producing endurance, and in making us complete and lacking nothing! Wow! Now that's a powerful promise!

Change your definition, considering it all joy, and watch your faith grow, your endurance increase, and your life become complete. You'll lack for nothing, simply because you've chosen to define things the way God defines them.

Belief consists in ccepting the ffirmations of the oul, unbelief in 'enying them."

–Ralph Waldo ;merson

Defining Things the Way God Defines Them

David is one of my heroes. He was one of Israel's greatest leaders, a man who developed a "heart after God's own heart." He faced many challenges, but he seemed to rise above each one! Even when the challenges were far bigger than he was, his perspective seemed to always carry him through. How was he able to do this? David was one who always defined things not as he saw them but as God saw them.

There was a day when David was still a young leader, and Israel was at war with the Philistines. Instead of the war being fought between both armies, they made a decision to choose the best, most spartan, warrior from each tribe and let the two of them duke it out. Each would represent their nation and would fight on behalf of their entire army. Whoever won would signify their nation's victory. Conversely, the nation of the one who lost would have to bear the consequences and become slaves to the nation of the winner.

A giant named Goliath was chosen to represent the Philistines. He towered over all the others, measuring over nine feet tall! His armor alone weighed over 100 pounds! I'll bet he was uglier than sin as well.

Goliath made such an impression that every Israelite warrior cowered in intimidation. The Bible reports, *"when all the men of Israel saw the man, they fled from him and were greatly afraid"* (1 Sam. 17:24). They would dart behind rocks, hide in caves, and duck behind bushes. Goliath would stand on a hill like a bully and taunt the Israelites, cursing them by his gods (1 Sam. 17:43).

David saw the taunting giant making fun of the trembling Israelites hiding in the thickets and behind bushes. He reviewed the situation and defined these Israelites as *"the armies of the Living God"*! (1 Sam. 17:26).

They sure didn't resemble "armies of a Living God"! They looked more like a bunch of chickens that just saw a fox, or a group of turkeys right before Thanksgiving. If David had described the situation according to how it looked he would have defined these men as wimps. Instead, he called them the "armies of the Living God"!

David could take this no longer. He walked up to this overgrown and unruly opponent and exclaimed:

> *"You come to me with a sword, a spear, and a javelin, but I come to you in the name of the Lord of Hosts, the God of the armies of Israel whom you have taunted" (1 Sam. 17:45).*

Righteous indignation filled his soul and courage flooded his veins. With five smooth stones in his bag, he loaded his slingshot and let it fly! His years of practice on the back side of the desert paid off, and the stone caught the giant right between the eyes. The Bible says, *"the stone sank into his forehead."*

The giant muttered something like, "Boy, nothing like this has ever entered my mind before" and fell on his face to the ground (1 Sam. 17:49).

(The muttering part is my paraphrase. You won't find it in your Bible, but it's in mine. I wrote it into the margin. It's the first case of a splitting headache ever recorded in the Bible.)

David chose to see things the way God saw them. And because he made this critical choice, God was able to use him to conquer impossible circumstances and lead His people to an overwhelming victory against the Philistines. So great is this victory of David over Goliath, that we still speak of it even today.

A second example of David defining things as God does is found in 1 Samuel 24. At this time, David was running from the wicked King Saul who wanted to take the young warrior's life. Saul's short-lived gratefulness to David for slaying Goliath turned into a long-term jealousy. Although David was innocent, Saul's insecurity drove him to rid his throne of any competitors. Saul's fears were obvious, yet David kept looking for the best in Saul, in spite of the problems.

It was in the cave of Engedi where David displayed a quality of leadership that was to become a hallmark of his life. David was hiding in the cave when Saul entered, unaware of David's presence. Weary from his pursuit of David, Saul fell asleep.

David's chance to rid himself of Saul's merciless crusade against him was within reach, and his men urged him on:

> *"'Behold, this is the day of which the Lord said to you, 'Behold; I am about to give your enemy into your hand, and you shall do to him as it seems good to you.". David said to his men, 'Far be it from me because of the Lord that I should do this thing to my lord, the Lord's anointed, to*

stretch out my hand against him, since he is the Lord's anointed.'" (1 Sam. 24:4, 6, emphasis mine).

Let me ask you, did Saul deserve to be called the "Lord's anointed"? Did he act like the Lord's anointed? Obviously not!

But then again, did the Israelites, dismayed from a bully's threats and fleeing in every direction, resemble the "army of the Living God"? Surely a misnomer! Why did God give David victory over his enemies? Why did God use him and make him Israel's greatest leader?

Here's the gem: David chose to define things as *God defined them!*

David became a ıan after God's ›wn heart because ıe defined events he way God !efined them."

—Wayne Cordeiro

David chose to see circumstances and events from God's perspective, and in doing so, he received God's strength and courage. His "eye was clear" (Mt. 6:22). His perspective was God-pleasing. This is why God made him successful in all he did. That kind of strength comes as a result of having the right attitude!

David became a man after God's own heart because he defined events the way God defined them.

Messing Up Inside the Father's House

Many Christians suffer from the malady of an attitude trained by their circumstances rather than by the Spirit of God. When that happens, we begin to resemble the elder brother in the story of the prodigal son found in Luke 15. His younger brother had taken his inheritance and squandered it, and now after seeing the error of his ways, returned home. Their father, overwhelmed with the joy of his prodigal son's return and repentance, called his elder son to rejoice with him.

"Many Christians suffer from the malady of an attitude trained by their circumstances rather than by the Spirit of God."

—Wayne Cordeiro

> *"But he became angry and was not willing to go in; and his father came out and began entreating him. But he answered and said to his father, 'Look! For so many years I have been serving you, and I have never neglected a command of yours; and yet you have never given me one young goat, that I might be merry with my friends. But when this son of yours came, who has devoured your wealth with harlots, you killed the fattened calf for him'" (Lk. 15:28-30).*

Sounds like sour grapes, doesn't it?

The prodigal indeed messed up his life *outside* the Father's house. However, because of a bad attitude, his elder brother messed up his life *inside* the Father's house.

Instead of looking for what he could be grateful for, he found a reason that could justify his anger. You see, if you look hard enough and wait long enough, you can always find reasons to justify complaints. If you compare yourself against others often enough, and investigate what's fair or unfair, you will surely find your "rights" offended somewhere along the line.

Looking for what is bad and not for the good causes each of us to develop a deadly cancer known as *ungratefulness*. It affects our attitude in subtle ways that may not surface for years. And this is what surfaced finally in the prodigal son's brother. Because of his attitude, which was focused on himself, he couldn't see the situation the way his father saw it. Because of his bad attitude, he couldn't welcome back his brother and he missed the blessing.

We can begin to do the same thing sometimes. Where, instead of seeing things as our Father sees them, and welcoming home a wayward brother or sister, we can begin to judge or complain, saying, "Hey what about me? What about all this time that I've been faithful?"

Our behavior can ause us to mess p our lives utside *the 'ather's house.)ur attitude will ause us to mess p our lives* inside *he Father's ouse."*

–Wayne Cordeiro

Our Father wants us to join Him in welcoming back those who have suffered outside His house. More importantly, He wants to make sure that our heart is right so we won't miss the blessing.

Our behavior can cause us to mess up our lives *outside* the Father's house. Our attitude will cause us to mess up our lives *inside* the Father's house.

Both are devastating.

Learning to Cultivate a Grateful Spirit

> *"In everything give thanks for this is the will of God for you in Christ Jesus" (1 Thes. 5:18, emphasis mine).*

Cultivate a spirit of gratefulness, regardless of the results ... not just when things are going your way, but in everything! Grateful attitudes never develop automatically. We must cultivate them and train them according to God's directions, much like programming a computer. If we set ourselves up with the right programming, we'll get the right results. Wrong programming, wrong results. No programming, no results. We get to "program" our attitudes with gratitude so that we can reap wonderful results.

"No one keeps up his enthusiasm automatically. Enthusiasm must be nourished with new actions, new aspirations, new efforts, new vision. It is one's own fault if his enthusiasm is gone. He has failed to feed it."

—Anonymous

You see, gratefulness is a spirit. It is not a response to gifts and favors given to you. Learn the secret of being thankful for what God has already done for you, regardless of how it may appear to you right now. Cultivate this spirit before you receive any favors, before you win the sweepstakes, before others are kind to you.

We find in the book of Psalm 16:6, *"The lines have fallen to me in pleasant places."* And again in Psalm 65:4, *"We will be satisfied with the goodness of Thy house, Thy holy temple."*

David wrote these lines of gratitude even in the midst of being a fugitive, hiding from a king intent on killing him. That's because David was satisfied with the way God was treating him in that season of his life. Though he was running from Saul, he was grateful for the protection and the sustaining hand of God. The "lines" that had fallen to him in pleasant places signified the fact that David knew he had limitations on his life. There were things out of his control and jurisdiction, yet he was grateful. The parameters or the limitations God placed on him were pleasant. You see, David's perspective on life, his attitude of excellence, is what gave him the edge.

You and I can cultivate the same kind of attitude. Life is like a garden. You will only grow what you cultivate. Gratefulness will come when you cultivate it in the soil of your life.

"Worse than being blind would be to be able to see but not have any vision."

—Helen Keller

Take the Time to Appreciate

One of the seven natural wonders of the world is the Grand Canyon. It is one of the most awe-inspiring sights in the world, stretching for miles on end. It is like God scooped out a vast divide with His hand and sprinkled hues of beautiful rainbow colors indelibly etching them into the granite and rocks. You can stand on the rim of the canyon and observe the eagles soaring beneath you. It truly is one of God's greatest masterpieces this side of heaven.

Some years ago, I took some kids from a youth group in Oregon on a trip to experience the Grand Canyon. Our journey involved 80 screaming kids jam-packed into seven vans. I had been driving for two days to show them this phenomenal, outstanding view of one of the earth's greatest natural wonders.

After an arduous journey, we finally arrived. Tired, but filled with anticipation, I was more excited for the kids than anything else. I had experienced this spectacular sight before, but for many of the kids, it would be their first time.

We jumped out of the van and hurried to the lookout point. Stepping up to the observation railing, we were immediately met by a hot thermal rushing over our faces. The wind blew our hair straight back, and we could see the eagles soaring. "Wow!" I thought. "This is *beautiful*! I could stay here all day!"

After three or four minutes, the kids looked at me and said, "All right! That was nice. Let's go!"

I said, "Let's go? Look at this view. It's beautiful!"

"Yeah, it's nice, Wayne, really nice. Now, let's go find a McDonald's."

I screamed, "Wait! You kids will stay here. You will enjoy this. You will remain here and enjoy this for at least ten minutes. I did not travel for two solid days to leave after three minutes and go to McDonald's! You will like this! You will open your eyes and just look!"

What I may have failed to realize was that these kids had been raised on television and they had seen the Grand Canyon many times before ... through the technological wonders of television. They had watched as a video camera mounted to a hang glider's aluminum frame zoomed through the Grand Canyon. They had viewed this natural wonder, through the lens of his camera, as he slid through the thermals and floated over the canyon, capturing a million different views and camera angles.

They had also seen it through the lens of history as a geologist allowed them the vantage point of his mind's eye. They might have seen it from the rafts of a whitewater excursion, cutting through the canyon's river canopied beneath the varicolored cathedral rising above.

This was their first *actual* experience, standing at a lookout point. Compared to the rest, I guess it wasn't all that great! It was only one narrow viewpoint.

A book of Jewish writings called the "Talmud" says, "God is going to hold us accountable for all the things that He put on this earth for us to enjoy and we didn't take time to do so."

"The foolish man seeks happiness in the distance, the wise grows it under his feet."

—James Oppenhiem

In training your eyes to see what is good, take the time to enjoy the simple things again. Pause long enough to smell the flowers. Stop long enough to sit down and see the sunrise or the sunset. Cultivate gratefulness. When you do, you'll begin to condition your attitude, cultivate a grateful spirit, and you will soon have a garden blooming with contentment.

Our Father has surrounded us with opportunities for joy. Enjoy the ride!

Learning to Enjoy the Ride!

One of the ways the Lord has trained my heart to cultivate gratefulness is in learning to enjoy this ride called life. There are going to be challenges and hills to climb in this journey. That's a given. Once you know that hills and trials will always be there, you'll be able to expect them, which will free you up and enable you to enjoy the ride.

"Our Father has surrounded us with opportunities for joy."

—Wayne Cordeiro

God created things for us to enjoy. Stop and enjoy them. Enjoy life. Enjoy the sunshine. Enjoy the rain. When you go home, enjoy your meal. When your wife says, "Mow the lawn!" enjoy mowing the lawn! Take the dog for a walk. Enjoy the walk and enjoy your time with your dog. This life is too short for us to not enjoy it. Enjoy the ride.

The Bible says, *"...The joy of the Lord is your strength" (Neh. 8:10)*. We can limp weakly through life because we have forgotten to take our joy. He has packed it for us but we can forget to take it along. In every activity you attend, carry along a wonderful pack of joy. Otherwise, you'll miss it.

"One filled with joy preaches without preaching."

—Mother Theresa

One summer, our family went to Disneyland. One of the rides my son wanted me to check out was the "Indiana Jones" ride. I said, "Let's go for it!"

I'm an analytical person and I watch stuff. As we were going through the line I said, "See that, Aaron. See that little creature on the rock? It's not really a creature at all. It's a mechanical device that's computer activated."

"Really?" he asked.

"Yeah! And see the shapes on the wall? They're made by a light being projected through a special filter. That filter's called a 'gobo.' See it?"

"Oh, yeah!" said Aaron, "Cool. Cool."

Spurred further by his interest I continued, "See that rock face over there ... with the mist gliding across it? That's smoke coming from a machine, not really morning mist at all."

Be still, and know that I am God...

(Psalm 46:10)

"Really?"

"Yeah. And see that over there, son?"

"Uh huh."

"That's a mirror."

"Really?"

We climbed into the car. "Do you see how this jeep is painted to look old, Aaron?"

"Yeah."

"It's brand new, though. Check out the serial number."

"Yeah, it is!"

"And look under the dash. There aren't any wires. You know why? Because it's on a track." As I was transforming into a combination of Mr. Spock and Sherlock Holmes, the jeep lunged forward and we were in motion. The speed increased and we whipped around a corner eliciting screams from the girls in the car next to us.

"That was good, Aaron, but if it was at another ten degrees, the G-force would have been better. It really would have made your stomach drop."

"Great, Dad," said Aaron, having to scream in order to be heard.

"You see that, Aaron? That's another mirror," I yelled, as we zipped down the track.

By this time, Aaron wasn't responding to my evaluations. He was in mid-flight with his head and body being jostled, twisted, and pulled with every turn of the track.

"See that rock coming at us? It's on a track," I yelled. "It'll go back and get reset for the next car behind us. Not very effective, huh?"

Before we realized it, the jeep came to a halt and the ride was over. "You know, Aaron, another thing is if we could have made a sharper turn on that second hairpin, it would've been even better. And if the smoke would've come out sooner, we could have traveled right through it instead of it passing us on the side."

Aaron stopped me in a less than gracious tone, "Hey, Dad, enough!"

"What do you mean, 'Enough!'?" Without answering, he turned and walked off. "Hey, you get over here. I've got more things to tell you," I called after him. He kept walking.

"Now is the time to love. Tomorrow the baby won't need to be rocked, the toddler won't be asking 'Why?' The schoolboy won't need help with his lessons, nor will he bring his school friends home for some fun. Tomorrow the teenager will have made his major decisions."

—John Dresches

"Enough!" he called back. "I ain't riding with you no more!"

"Okay. I'll meet you later!" I answered. Then under my breath I muttered to myself, "Dumb kid! He just doesn't listen, does he? That's his problem."

As I was walking around kicking the dirt, the Lord spoke to my heart, "You missed the whole ride, didn't you? You were so busy trying to figure everything out, you missed the whole ride."

I stopped and thought, "You know, that's right! I don't even remember the ride! I was so involved in all the little details I missed the whole ride!"

Have you ever done that? Have you ever gotten so caught up in the details of life that before you know it, the ride is over? Life is done? Ever get so caught up in the preparations of a wedding that you miss the wedding? Ever get so distracted with cleaning the house before guests arrive that you alienate your whole family in the process?

How often we get short with others, blame our families, and hiss at our neighbors. We're so distracted with the "little details" we forget to enjoy the ride! We miss the beauty of the sunrises and sunsets, our children grow up without us, and the beauty of this ride called "life" goes unnoticed.

My own children have grown up so quickly! It seems like they were in diapers just a few minutes ago. Then all too quickly they were walking across the platform to receive their high school diplomas. The next minute they're gone. The ride is over!

We're like Martha, in Luke 10:40, who was so *"distracted with all her preparations"* that she began to complain. Turning to the Lord, she exploded, *"Lord, do You not care that my sister has left me to do all the serving alone? Then tell her to help me."*

We begin our days with a jolt of coffee, motor from task to task, return home exhausted, only to get up and do it all over again.

"God has given us a beautiful world to live in filled with His wonders, His people and Himself. It's there, if we'll only take the time to enjoy it."

—Wayne Cordeiro

Instead of missing the ride, instead of just driving through at a relentless pace, let's slow down. Instead of missing the beauty of this process called "life," let's *enjoy the ride.* God has given us a beautiful world to live in filled with His wonders, His people and Himself. It's there, if we'll only take the time to enjoy it.

It's taken me awhile to learn this essential lesson. And I'm so glad I caught it. Here are a few ways I've learned to enjoy the ride:

1. Take five minutes today and write down the names of two people you appreciate. They may be people that have gone unnoticed. It could be a spouse, a friend, or someone who did a good deed in the past and it slipped by everyone's notice. Write them a note of thanks. Be sure to add as much detail as you can about how that person's actions blessed you. And send it!
2. Don't forget to laugh. Some of us need to learn to laugh again. There is plenty to laugh about in life. And we need to laugh. Stand naked in front of a mirror. That alone should take care of your laughter quota for a day or two.

   Keep record of how many times you laugh today. It could be for any reason at all, but try to get it up to at least five times! You'll find great opportunities by listening to children or spend a few more minutes in the lunchroom with your co-workers. If that's not working, go into the bathroom (again!) and imagine you're entering a funny face contest. Practice before a mirror. (Be sure no one else is in the restroom at the same time! You might check all the stalls before proceeding.)

3. Do one thing for yourself today. Write it into your schedule. Often I will stop on the way home at a little yogurt shop for a frozen dessert. It takes only about 15 minutes for me to lick that thing to its end, but oh the ecstasy of those few minutes. It slows me down before I arrive home. For you it could be a short jog, a walk, or listening to some of your favorite music. Whatever it is, take time to enjoy life in its simplest form.

4. Make a new friend today. If you had an assignment to make a new friend, how would you do it? This may only take a few minutes to stop and truly be interested in another person's life. Ask that person about his or her family, dreams, or struggles. Then listen. Truly listen. You'll be surprised how many friends you will collect over a period of just a few days!

> By the way, a great place to start is with your family. You'll be surprised how many of us are related, but not friends. Life is too short for that. By establishing deep friendships with your family, you'll begin to reap one of God's greatest promises and rewards.

Pause long enough to enjoy the ride. Train yourself to see what is good. Take the time to laugh with each other. Laugh at yourself. Although there will be imperfections and periodic setbacks, you will be surprised how wonderful life can be with a good attitude. You will hear God better. You will enjoy His presence.

You will be pleasantly surprised how it will help you to develop an attitude that attracts friends, laughter, joy, and success!

CHAPTER FOUR

Raising the Bar of Excellence

"A dull axe requires great strength. Be wise and sharpen the blade." (Ecclesiastes 10:10)

Developing your attitude is like developing your skill on a musical instrument: it takes consistent practice to improve.

"Character: the commitment to carry out a worthy decision long after the emotion of making that decision has passed."

—Wayne Cordeiro

When the great pianist, Paderewski, was elected to become Prime Minister to his country, he made one request before he accepted the prestigious office. He would lead the country but he must be allowed to practice his scales for two hours every day.

The guitar virtuoso, Andres Segovia, requires the same of his students: two hours a day playing scales.

Now who plays scales in a concert? You've never heard a composition by Mozart or Brahms called the "Aeolian Scale" or the "Major Scale." However, without being thoroughly familiar with each scale, a musician would remain remedial in his or her art. It is the complete mastery of the basics which gives birth to a freedom of expression, an ease of movement, and a cohesiveness in the delivery of each phrase.

So it is with each of us in our attitudes. Though we may have excelled in the area of attitude, we need to continue to develop it each day. We need to practice having an excellent attitude in each and every endeavor. For it will always be true that each of us can excel still more in the way we see problems, people, and life.

Directly after World War II, General MacArthur went to Japan to evaluate the rebuilding of a war torn nation. The economy of Japan was in dire straits. Having to use leftover resources, Japan was struggling just to stay afloat. As a result, during the sixties, any toy or appliance that said, "Made in Japan" would signify one thing: poor quality. Realizing their dilemma, General MacArthur brought in one of America's best quality control experts, Dr. W. Edward Demming.

After much evaluation and scrutiny, he came up with a set of business principles to help turn the economy of Japan around. He called the most influential business owners together and offered them a promise. He said, "If you will improve something about yourself and your product every day, and make quality not merely something to be maintained but an achievement and a way of living, you will turn the economy of Japan around in ten years. Then if you continue to improve something each day, even if it is a miniscule amount, in three decades you will become an economic world power."

That was quite a tall promise to make to this struggling nation, but they took it, hook, line, and sinker. They even coined a new word for this, "kaizen." This means a constant, ever-increasing improvement that defines quality not as something to be maintained but something to be lived on a daily basis.

"A vision is a guidepost that keeps you on track with God's plan for your life."

—Kevin Baerg

Over the next ten years, the businesses of Japan did exactly that. They would take an American auto and improve it. Then they'd sell it back to American consumers. People began buying everything Japan produced because of the improved quality. Japanese ingenuity increased, as they learned from American models of appliances, electronic devices, tools, cameras, and watches. The Japanese constantly improved each one until their products were in demand the world over.

In ten years, the economy of Japan had reversed itself, and within three decades it had become an economic world power. Till this day, one of the most prestigious business awards presented on national television is the W. Edward Demming Award.

If Japan can do that for their nation's economy, how much more should we do it for the sake of the Kingdom of God!

For the Sake of the Kingdom

> *"We request of you, as you have received instruction as to how you ought to walk and please God, just as you actually do walk, that you may excel still more" (1 Thes. 4:1, emphasis mine).*

"Dream lofty dreams, and as you dream, so shall you become. Your vision is the promise of what you shall one day be."

—James Allen

What is Paul saying? Keep on improving for the sake of the Kingdom of God. Be willing to improve. Be willing to get better.

Even if it means 1 percent a day, improve something about yourself. Sharpen something! If you can improve just 1 percent a day, that means over one year you will have improved over 300 percent for the Kingdom of God. Just 1 percent a day! Improve something about yourself! It may be the way you stand, comb your hair, or something to improve your hygiene. It could be the way you shake people's hands, the way to look at people in the eye when you talk with them. Whatever it might be, improve something. It may be your posture or your speech. Instead of saying, "Yeah. Okay..." say, "Sure, I would love to!" When someone asks for your help, instead of replying, "I guess so," say, "I would be more than honored to help!"

"If you improve something about yourself 1% a day for one year, can you imagine how much you will grow? Raise the bar of excellence!"

—Wayne Cordeiro

Where can we improve? In the way I treat my spouse, the way I speak, in my faith, my discipline, or my attitude. Do something to *"excel still more"* for the sake of the Kingdom. Improve something about yourself 1 percent a day for one year, and imagine how much you will grow! Raise the bar!

Realizing the Potential Inside of You

During my collegiate years in Oregon, I played club soccer at the University of Oregon. The soccer field we would use for scrimmages happened to be in the middle of the university's track. In different sections on the surrounding track, various teams would be practicing the high jump, pole vault, triple jump, and other events. Incidentally, Eugene is a mecca for track and field events. In fact, that is where the Nike company got their start.

I remember being intrigued by a persistent high jumper. He was practicing for a prestigious track meet that was eight months away. The bar on the high jump was set at 5'9". Now, 5'9" is taller than I am, so for me that is high! He made his attempt and cleared it. I looked at him and thought, "Wow! That's amazing! No springs, no pogo stick, he just jumped!"

"If you can dream it, you can do it."

—Walt Disney

If I ever cleared the bar at 5'9", I would retire. I would take a picture of myself next to the height of the bar, buy myself the biggest trophy I could afford, and brag to my kids forever. Not this athlete. Instead of retiring, he raised the bar and jumped again.

He jumped 5'10" and instead of being satisfied, he raised the bar again. He did this for eight months!

Finally, the day of the track meet arrived. I bought a ticket for the event just to watch this high jumper who had become the object of my interest over the past eight months. The meet was packed, and the high jump competition began. Many of the high jumpers started faulting out, failing to clear the bar at 6'1" and 6'2". Finally, the metal bar was set at 6'4". My high jumper was the final contestant. He would be given three chances to clear 6'4", and if he did, he would win the high jump competition.

After they reset the bar, he launched his first attempt. He hit the bar, falling to the ground with the bar in tow. In his second attempt, he again dislodged the bar. The crowd grew nervous with anticipation as he faced his third, and final, attempt.

I can still recall him consulting his coach—about the thrust of his head, the arch of his back and the timing of his foot. When he had mentally gone through each step and every necessary maneuver, he returned to the field. He stared at the bar as if he were striking a deal with it.

After what seemed like an eternity, he nodded slightly, and started his long, semi-circular run toward the bar. Then with every ounce of his conditioned strength and power, he planted one foot into the ground and launched into his final jump. Every tendon and joint stretched tight as he catapulted his body into the air. He thrust his head toward the clouds, his back arched in a precise curve over the top of the bar, his foot flicked at the precise moment, and he began his descent. *He cleared the bar!*

"God brings His vision to fulfillment not through our strength, but by His strength working in us."

—Randy Phillips

His teammates rushed out of the grandstands cheering. Caught up in the emotion of the moment, I found myself crying and running towards the champion saying, "You don't even know me but I want to give you a hug!"

This was amazing to me! I remember him attempting to clear 5'9". But all the while, there was inside of him the potential of 6'4"! *Yet he would never have realized that potential unless he had been willing to raise the bar.*

Some of us are jumping at 2'6". We figure that's good enough. God says, "Inside of you, there is the potential of 6'4". What are you doing at 2'6"?"

Some of you might say, "Not me! I'm a 2'6" kind of person!" But God is saying there is so much more inside you! Much more! In order to achieve that, you must be willing to raise the bar.

God is not saying to raise the bar a foot at a time. He is saying, one inch is fine. This is incrementally increasing your abilities. Keep improving yourself for the sake of the Kingdom of God, whether it be the depth of your faith, the way you treat people, or the way you think. Improve these 1 percent every day. You know what will happen? The very potential God has wired up inside of you will begin to emerge because it is in there.

But, first, you must be willing to raise the bar.

Break through Quitting Points

"Great minds have purposes; others have wishes."

—Washington Irving

One of the things that wars against *"excelling still more"* is our individual quitting points. These are points where we give up. This is where someone tests your patience to a certain limit and you say, "That's it!" This can happen in our patience with our children, in our fight against temptation, or in our moral code. Every single one of us has quitting points. What are some of your quitting points?

Maybe it's in relationships. When things are smooth, everything's fine. What happens when the temperature begins to rise and you don't see eye to eye on things like you used to? The mercury on the thermometer rises above normal and we feel the heat. Finally it gets to be 104 degrees and you say, "That's it! I'm not taking this anymore. I'm out of here!"

At a certain level of pain, we reach our quitting point, and our systems shut down. This quitting point can be the result of past habits or simply our predetermined tolerance levels for problem solving. Nevertheless, we bail out with predictable consistency, right at that certain quitting point.

"Our attitude is the primary force that will determine whether we succeed or fail."

—John Maxwell

On a pain threshold of one to ten, with one being "no pain at all" and ten being "extremely painful," how do you do? When something gets to be a four, is that your quitting point? When someone gives us trouble or doesn't accept our suggestions. When things don't go exactly the way we want them to, we start counting, "One. Two. Three. Four! That's it! I'm through!" And we bail at our quitting point.

The devil is very shrewd, he may be defeated, but he's not stupid. He is crafty and deceptive, and he would love nothing better than to take down as many of God's children as he can before his time is up. He knows your quitting points.

I'll bet Satan has statistical records on each of us like a college football coach keeps on all the players of the opposing teams. He has a file with your name on it, and in this file is a graph plotting all your common quitting points. He keeps tally of all these things. The devil knows that on a pain threshold of one to ten, at 5.5 you bail out every time. Now he has your number. How does he use that information against you?

He's Got Your Number

The devil knows that whatever you need to do to sidestep pain or consequences, you'll do it. Even if it means to go against your faith, your family, or your future. If you are unwilling to break through quitting points, you will have a tendency to let the avoidance of pain become your god. Now all the devil needs to do is cause some rumblings and some seismic activity so it gets increasingly worse in a relationship. It could begin with a complaint you've received or a criticism about your weight or performance. It could be the loss of someone close to you that you refuse to release. This may be further exacerbated by a financial or health setback. Whatever the case, soon the thermometer reaches 104, and we all know what's coming up next. Some people bail out, some people blow up in anger, some use it as an excuse to dive into the bottle, an affair, or into drugs.

"Success is not measured by how you do compared to how somebody else does. Success is measured by how you do compared to what you could have done with what God gave you."

—Zig Ziglar

One of the methods by which a man or a woman is measured is determined by what it takes to get him or her to bail out of a commitment. That could be a commitment to a marriage, a commitment of his or her faith, a commitment of a friendship, or a commitment to a home church. What is the threshold of your quitting point?

> *"For you have need of* endurance, *for after you have done the will of*

> *God, you will receive what was promised" (Heb. 10:36, emphasis mine).*

Circle the word "endurance" in your heart and mind. For you have need of endurance to break through those quitting points and keep going in the same direction. If, in the past, you exploded at 104 degrees, make a decision now for that to change. Increase your capacity to deal with problems and you will be surprised how much more fruitful life will be.

Pay the Price to Build Character

Another important aspect of developing an excellent attitude is found in the depth of our character formation. The deeper the character, the easier it is to develop an attitude of excellence. Without character, there is no foundation in your life.

How do we develop character?

> *"By this is My Father glorified, that you bear much fruit, and so prove to be My disciples" (Jn. 15:8).*

Sometimes, we want the good things of life handed to us on a silver platter. But, there is a price to pay for godly character. God is developing in you the necessary character in order to be fruitful in your relationships, finances, and spiritual maturity. Character is required as the

"Character is a victory, not a gift."
—Ivor Griffith

foundation. Without it, you will never survive success.

Although God desires success for each of us, success has inherent points that will make you vulnerable. If there is a shallowness of character, you will fall prey to the clutches of pride, avarice, greed, or the abuse of power.

Imagine you owned a four-karat diamond worth thousands of dollars. That beautiful diamond would be delicately displayed by a setting made up of five or six fingers called "prongs." If the prongs were soft and prone to bending, a qualified jeweler would never mount such a stone into this weak setting. One sharp bump and the diamond would be lost forever. The value of the ring would be drastically reduced.

The jeweler must work diligently on the setting. When the diamond is polished and set, the fingers of the setting tightly grasp the stone. The setting not only displays the radiant beauty of the diamond, but it also holds it fast. Even when the ring is bumped, the strong fingers won't let go.

Character is like the setting of a ring. If we don't allow God to build strong character, then we won't be ready for the success He wants to bring to our lives. Character doesn't come cheap. It comes at a price: the price of digging your knees into the carpet, the price of studying, the price of suffering, and the price of going through trials and discipline.

We must be willing to pay the price. Let's look at what Paul says in the book of Philippians:

> *"Everything else is worthless when compared with the priceless gain of knowing Christ Jesus my Lord,* so whatever it takes *I will be one who lives in the fresh newness of life" (Philip. 3:8, 11 LB, emphasis mine).*

Circle those three words in your heart: "whatever it takes." Whatever it takes, be willing to pay the price for character. And whatever it takes, let's be counted among those who live in the fresh newness of life!

To Feel Good about Yourself: Stay Clean!

I'm not talking about body odor. I'm talking about sin in your life. You can't feel good about yourself while living in sin. There just isn't any way. You also cannot feel good about yourself when you're tolerating sin. You must repent as often as you need in order to stay clean. Don't tolerate unresolved sin. Remember! It's not sin that destroys God's people, necessarily, it's unresolved sin!

"It's not sin that destroys God's people, necessarily, it's unresolved sin!"

—Wayne Cordeiro

> *"If I regard wickedness in my heart, the Lord will not hear me" (Ps. 66:18).*

In the book of Joshua a man named Achan sinned by stealing things he knew were not his to take. Nevertheless, he proceeded with his sin and then hid it. He figured that if no one knew, then nobody would be hurt.

The following day, Israel went back out to battle and were duly routed by the enemy. Joshua was confused because he knew God had promised them victory over their enemies. Why were they defeated? He questioned God, who answered, *"Israel sinned ... therefore, the sons of Israel cannot stand before their enemies"* (Josh. 7:11-12).

Further investigation revealed that Achan had indeed disobeyed God's commands, and his unresolved sin was causing their weakness in battle. It wasn't until Achan's sin was cleaned from their camp that the Israelites once again returned to victory. You see, unresolved sin in your camp can cause you to miss out on God's blessings.

..Let us also lay ıside every ·ncumbrance, and he sin which so ·asily entangles ıs, and let us run with endurance he race that is set ·efore us...

(HEBREWS 12:1)

Unresolved sin steals your confidence and causes you to have an attitude of defeatism and fear. Don't tolerate unresolved sin! Stay clean, and repent as often as you need to stay in the flow of God's blessings.

Justifying Ourselves

One way we attempt to resolve sin is by renaming it. We change the word *sin* to something more tolerable.

"It's an 'alternative lifestyle.' What's wrong with being gay?"

"It's a 'domestic partnership.'"

"Hey, sure we live together, but we really love each other and plan to get married some day."

Let me share with you why this line of thinking is so dangerous. You see, there is no forgiveness for domestic partnerships. There's no forgiveness for alternative lifestyles or being gay. There's no forgiveness for living together. *There's only forgiveness for sin.* Until we say it's sin, forgiveness is not available. Can you see how important this is? Can you see the subtle strategy of the enemy to take the word "sin" and color it over and obscure it? Then we wouldn't need forgiveness because we have justified it. However, forgiveness is not available until we confess it as "sin."

And Peter said to them, "Repent, and let each of you be baptized in the name of Jesus Christ for the forgiveness of your sins; and you shall receive the gift of the Holy Spirit."

(Acts 2:38)

> *"If we confess our sins, He is faithful and righteous to forgive us our sins and to cleanse us from all unrighteousness" (1 Jn. 1:9).*

Okay, but no one is perfect. We all slip here or there. Does that disqualify us? How do we keep clean?

Keeping a Clean House

If I told you my wife keeps a clean house, that wouldn't mean it never gets dirty. That would be impossible! Why? Because we have three kids! What I'm saying is this: although our house gets messy, it doesn't stay that way very long until it gets cleaned up. When it does get messy again, it is soon restored back to order.

The same is true with you. Though we might stumble, fumble and fall, don't tolerate any unresolved situation. Don't live with it or let it stay that way for a long time. Clean it. You'll stumble. Clean it. You'll make a mistake. Clean it. You can't develop a godly attitude when you're living in unresolved sin. Stay clean!

Hudson Taylor was a missionary to China. He understood the importance of staying clean. He knew that a repenting person was a healthy person. A repenting church would be a healthy church. This was so important to him that when he greeted people during the day, he wouldn't shake their hand and ask, "How are you today?" Instead, he'd shake their hand and ask, "Have you repented today?" It wasn't an attempt to condescend, but a sincere expression of encouraging people to stay clean!

God has much forgiveness for you. Forgiveness is abundantly available for sin. If it's sin, say, "Lord, forgive me of my sin." God will not condemn you. He will invite you into His forgiveness. God never speaks to you in words of condemnation. He'll always speak to you with words of invitation. That's the kind of God we serve.

Don't ever believe the lies of the devil that will try to cause you to define God as a bad guy. God loves you! He died for you! Does that tell you how valuable you are? So, stay clean.

CHAPTER FIVE

Play the Right Background Music

"...Speaking to one another in psalms and hymns and spiritual songs, singing and making melody with your heart to the Lord." (Ephesians 5:19)

God created every human being with a built-in music system. It resembles the "music-on-hold" you hear when you are waiting to talk to your doctor, or the music that wafts through the mall to entice you to shop more.

Our internal music is composed of the thoughts we think about over and over. They can include selected memories—maybe something your mom or dad once said to you, maybe an encouragement from a teacher, or an experience when you weren't picked to be on the team or to be someone's friend. As you dwell on certain memories, experiences, and thoughts, they are recorded on the soundtrack of your mind and play continuously all day long.

Whatever you play affects everything about you. It affects your attitude, your self-image, your confidence level, your relationships, the way you communicate with others, and even your faith.

Each of us gets to determine what music we are going to play on our individual systems. You are the disc jockey, and you choose your own theme songs. Doesn't that seem wonderful? We get to play the most beautiful music of our selection to accompany us throughout our day. We could have any grand soundtrack or opera or melodious composition that we so desire!

Whatever is true, whatever is honorable, whatever is right, whatever is pure, whatever is lovely, whatever is of good repute, if there is any excellence and if anything worthy of praise, let your mind dwell on these things.

(PHILIP. 4:8)

The reality is that many of us play the wrong music. Some of our tapes and CDs have scratches on them. Some are so old, they're like the 78 rpm vinyl records of years ago—old tapes, old songs, and old experiences that should long have been forgotten (or forgiven).

Some people have been playing the same songs repeatedly for years. Their theme songs resemble these tunes: "It's my party and I'll cry if I want to..." Or, "Put your head on my shoulder..." Or, "What kind of fool am I?"

What is it that really makes a motion picture? Isn't it the music! Try watching "Jaws" with the sound turned off. It's ridiculous! All you see is a rubber fish trying to jump onto sinking boats.

Then turn on the music! The repeating pattern of the score and the rhythmic pounding of the arrangement makes your blood curdle and your heart pumps in cadence with each beat. You begin to perspire when the string section crescendos, and when the horns blast, you take cover! Till this day I am still afraid of any body of water for fear that Jaws may be present! I even refuse to take baths in my tub as a direct, dysfunctional result of my movie-going.

These memories hang on for a long time if you'll let them. They will play the selections attached to them, giving you feelings of fear or courage, insecurity or assurance.

You are the disc jockey. What is your play list? You get to make the selection, so do it now!

Steward Your Memories Well

"All meaningful and lasting change starts on the inside and works its way out."

—Bob Moawad

One thing that can act as a major impediment to developing a great attitude is the way we steward our memories. Past experiences, as well as our perceptions of those experiences, are collected over the years. These are stored in what I call our internal photo album. Here your memories, like pictures, are catalogued for quick retrieval.

These photo albums are similar to the ones we keep on the shelves in our family room. Those albums are filled with pictures of our children, vacations, birthday parties, graduations, and the like. The pictures that made it into these hallowed pages of fame represent only a fraction of the pictures actually taken. How did these specific pictures get the honor of holding the family's memories? What qualities gave each snapshot the privilege of being commemorated in the family photo album?

Well, it works like this. The family member who is the first to arrive on the scene and thumb through the pictures, recently returned from the photofinisher, becomes the judge of what pictures will actually make the cut. In our household, that person is usually me. (I plan it that way!)

Now the selection process begins. As I am thumbing through the 3 x 5 prints, if I come across a picture that makes me look heavier than I really am, out it goes! It is usually discarded immediately without a trial. If there's one that was snapped at the precise moment a fork full of food was entering my mouth, it enters the dark abyss of my trash can. If there's one that shows me with my eyes closed, looking funny, with bad posture, or anything else that might be conceived in the eyes of the beholder as less than optimum, it is whisked away without funeral or fuss.

Only those pictures that cause me to rival the best male models make it in! Then when someone pages through one of our family albums, I look like I just stepped off a Hollywood set.

Now, we would never allow all the pictures into our albums. That would be horrible.

And neither would we take the poorest of the pictures, place them neatly under each cellophane page, and throw away the best! That would be atrocious!

"Your imagination can focus on ugliness, distress and failure, or it can picture beauty, success, and desired results. You decide how you want your imagination to serve you."

—Philip Conley

As silly as that may be, that's often exactly what we do with memories. We forget the best and remember the worst. We tuck the injuries away in the pages of our photo albums and whenever we get the chance, we thumb through the pain again and again. If you flipped through the majority of people's memory albums, you'd probably find fewer prize pictures and many more painful ones.

Memories Give Courage or Steal Courage

Our memories are like pictures, and it is absolutely critical we steward them well. The reason? The memories you choose to keep will either give you courage or they will steal what you have. They will either help to build your faith or bring you doubts.

For example, if someone injured you in the past, you can either file that picture in your album or discard it. If you choose to *retain* and *rehearse* the event, turning it over and over in your mind, it will affect you adversely. Each time you come in contact with this person, you'll notice a distance has been growing between you. Your greatest attempts to make conversation will be shallow and insincere at best. The memory will have stolen your courage to solve the problem and interact genuinely. On the other hand, if you stored pictures of wonderful experiences, these would give you courage and build your faith.

David, as he faced his opponent Goliath, drew courage from his memories of what God had done for him in the past. This giant stood over nine feet tall and mocked the Israelites on the battlefield. The two warring nations had agreed that two warriors, one from each side, would settle the score between them. The winner would claim victory for his nation. Conversely, the one who lost would bring defeat to his side.

David confidently stood before King Saul and asked to be chosen for the task of defeating Goliath. Take a look at the following scriptures:

> *"And David said, 'Your servant has killed both the lion and the bear; and this uncircumcised Philistine will be like one of them, since he has taunted the armies of the living God. The Lord who delivered me from the paw of the lion and from the paw of the bear, He will deliver me from the hand of this Philistine.' And Saul said to David, 'Go, and may the Lord be with you'" (1 Sam. 17:36-37).*

"God is looking for those through whom He can do the possible—what a pity that we plan only the things that we can do by ourselves."

—A.W. Tozer

Where did this young lad find such courage and faith? From his photo album.

He remembered that the Lord had been with him when he killed the lion and the bear. And he knew that against the mighty Goliath, the Living God would deliver him again. His confidence was based on his experiences and his victorious memories.

Steward your memories well. What are you remembering? Are you stewarding your memories well or are you putting all the worst pictures into your album while discarding the best? Often we remember what we should forget, and we forget what we should remember.

"The brain is like a muscle. When we think well, we feel good."

—Carl Sagan, celebrity scientist

Maybe it's time to do some spring-cleaning! Go through the memories you've been keeping. Go through your old tapes and scratched CDs. Take a few moments to write down the pictures you need to discard. Evaluate them one by one. Do you need to bury the hatchet? Do you need to extend forgiveness? Then do so. And get rid of the bad memories!

Take a few minutes to get the balance back so that we forget what we should forget and remember what we should remember! Build up your best memories, memories that give you courage. And as you replace your old albums with victorious new memories you will begin to gain a new, God-given confidence, one that leads you to an excellent attitude. This one principle will be a basic you can practice in developing an attitude that attracts success!

Learning to Think Correctly

The way we steward what's happening on the inside will affect the way we think. If we think clearly, we'll have a better chance at having a healthy attitude towards the circumstances that come our way. If our thinking is poor, we'll have a tendency to develop a poor attitude.

The people who know their God will be strong and carry out great exploits.

(DAN. 11:32)

If that is true, then we must control the thoughts in our minds! Just because the thoughts are present, it doesn't mean they are correct.

M. Scott Peck in his book, "The People of the Lie," tells about one of the Vietnam War's greater tragedies, the "Mylai Massacre." It was on a morning in March of 1968, in the Quang Ngai Province of South Vietnam. Under the command of Lieutenant William Calley, hundreds of innocent women and children were killed randomly. The little village was known to have been harboring South Vietcong soldiers. However, when Task Force Barker arrived, they searched the village and found it was empty of soldiers. Yet having orders to take no chances, the soldiers rounded up groups of twenty to thirty at a time and with rifle fire or grenades, each group was routinely eliminated until the village had been eradicated.

Dr. Peck, a psychologist, was called in to investigate what would make men perform such acts of senseless violence. He interviewed the soldiers as well as the officers involved. His findings concluded that the massacre wasn't necessarily motivated by vindictive or evil intentions. It was simply due to an unwillingness to think deeply about what was going on. They had orders given by Lieutenant Calley, and without investigation or forethought for what the consequences may have been, they acted in a mindless, barbaric fashion.

Dr. Peck's conclusion gives us these poignant findings:

"As a people, we're too lazy to learn and too arrogant to think we needed to learn. We felt that whatever way we happened to perceive things was the right way without any further study. And whatever we did was the right thing to do without reflection."

Often our thoughts are the initial perceptions that come into our minds. These are not necessarily the correct conclusions, only the initial ones. To think that whatever comes into our minds about a person or situation is always the truth would indeed make us a "people of the lie."

If your thinking is poor, so will be your perspective. And if your perspective is poor, so will be your decisions.

Training Your Thoughts

John Wesley once quipped, "I can't stop a bird from flying over my head, but I sure can stop him from making a nest in my hair!"

What he was alluding to was the fact that although wrong thoughts may pass through my mind from time to time, I won't let them take up residence and give those wrong thoughts an audience. I may have little control over those fleeting thoughts, but I surely am responsible for the ones I allow to set up shop in my mind.

God requires each of us to judge and evaluate our thoughts and intentions. If they are not sound or biblical, then we must bring them into submission to God's Word. Just because a thought is lodged into your mind does not mean it belongs there! You must decide and steward the thoughts that are being housed in your heart and mind. If it doesn't fit into God's best, expel the thought!

"Imagination is more important than knowledge."
—Albert Einstein

> *"We use our powerful God-tools for smashing warped philosophies, tearing down barriers erected against the truth of God, fitting every loose thought and emotion and impulse into the structure of life shaped by Christ" (2 Cor. 10:5 The Message).*

In Ephesians 6:14-17, we find the armor of God articulated. Paul compares six pieces of the Roman armor to truths the believer can apply. Let's focus on this portion of Scripture's armor:

"Therefore put on the full armor of God, so that when the day of evil comes, you may be able to stand your ground, and after you have done everything, to stand. Stand firm therefore ... and take the helmet of salvation.*" (Eph. 6:13, 17, emphasis mine).*

One of the soldier's main pieces of protection is his helmet, which the Bible calls the "helmet of salvation." The Roman helmet was usually made of bronze or a bronze alloy. It was virtually impenetrable. It was fronted by a hinged visor to protect the soldier's facial area during battle. The helmet was designed to protect the neck as well, for in battle, the soldier's neck would be a prime target for an opponent who could easily decapitate him.

The application to each of us is that we must protect our thought life! If the adversary of our souls can find a Christian with an unprotected thought life, he has found his mark. Satan is a headhunter, our minds are the battlefield, and our imaginations are his trophies.

Protect yourself well, protecting your thought life and stewarding what goes on in your mind. Then you too will be able to stand your ground against Satan and against becoming a people of the lie. And in that way, when everything is done, you will be left standing victorious.

Your Belief Window

Hanging in front of every one of us is an invisible window through which we see everything. It's a glass pane, about two-foot square, attached to our head and hangs in front of our eyes. All through life, we view events and circumstances, people and problems through this belief window.

As time goes on, different things are etched onto our windows. Whatever is written will color or discolor what we are viewing through that window. It can either be something wonderful, like God's promises, or it can be demeaning, like a remembered insult. It can resemble a beautiful mural or bad graffiti, depending on what you choose to allow onto your window.

"You move toward and become like the thoughts you hold uppermost in your mind."

—Bob Moawad

Growing up, your parents may have drummed into you that you're slow or you're always irresponsible. Then from that time forward, you'll view everything in the light of that statement. "You'll never amount to anything," they may have said. Later in life should you make a mistake, you'll view that situation in such a way that confirms the fact that you indeed are irresponsible and slow.

You can't always do anything about people spraying graffiti on your window, but you can do something about letting what they write remain there!

You alone are responsible for the cleaning of that window ... inside as well as out! You see, we have a tendency to scribble some pretty demeaning things on it ourselves! You must steward that window and assure that only those things which build you up remain there. The Bible tells us in 1 Thessalonians 5:11, *"Therefore encourage one another, and build up one another..."*

God's Word: Our Window Cleaner

One of the best ways to ensure your thoughts are correct is to judge them by God's Word, the Bible. If God wouldn't say it to you, then off it comes without another thought given to it. Don't hold a funeral for it and don't dwell on it. If it doesn't build you up, *"whoosh!"* out it goes!

Discipline yourself to have a daily time reading the Scriptures, even if for a few minutes. It is God's Word that will keep your belief window clean and your thoughts healthy. And healthy thoughts build healthy attitudes!

There is nothing that can equal the benefit of reading the Bible on a consistent basis. If the devil can keep you from the Word, he can keep you from realizing your full potential in life.

> *"All Scripture is inspired by God and profitable for teaching, for reproof, for correction, for training in righteousness; that the man of God may be adequate, equipped for every good work" (2 Tim. 3:16).*

Let God's Word clean your perspective and mentor you in the ways of life. It will form your character and fashion your personality. It will shape your attitude until it becomes the underlying foundation for fruitfulness in every area of your life. Remember, poor thoughts equal poor attitudes.

> *"The lamp of the body is the eye; if therefore your eye is clear, your whole body will be full of light" (Mt. 6:22).*

God's Word tells us that the lamp of our body is our eyes. What does that mean? I looked up the word "lamp" in my dictionary and here's the definition: "a device that generates light ... for the purpose of illumination." A secondary definition said a lamp is "something that illumines the mind or soul." Wow! I liked that definition even better.

Jesus compared our eyes to lamps because they illuminate our mind and our soul. He knew we receive all of our information through these vessels. So whatever was illuminated into our mind, however we viewed the world, became our thoughts. He also knew that whatever became our thoughts had the power to affect our very soul. That's why He says, *"if therefore your eye is clear, your whole body will be full of light."* Because He knew we simply had to keep our eyes clear in order to have a life filled with light.

Isn't it time we *"trim the lamps"* of our bodies as Matthew 6:22 tells us? Isn't it time each of us does some spring cleaning in the attics of our minds in order to develop attitudes that attract success? Let God reveal the improper ways we think and cooperate with Him as we trim our lamps!

> *"Let us therefore, as many as are perfect, have this attitude; and if in anything you have a different attitude, God will reveal that also to you" (Philip. 3:15).*

Building Right Treasures

> *"Watch over your heart with all diligence, for from it flow the springs of life" (Pr. 4:23).*

Proverbs gives us a gem of a truth we would do well to carefully consider. If we miss this or fail to understand its truth, it would be like having a powerful car with an Indianapolis 500 engine, except the driver didn't know how to drive! Our heart is the seat from which all of life is affected, positively or negatively. And when we understand the immense power of our hearts, we as the drivers of that vehicle will be better able to operate it.

We find in Matthew 12:34-35 these words: *"For the mouth speaks out of that which fills the heart. The good man out of his good treasure brings forth what is good; and the evil man out of his evil treasure brings forth what is evil."*

What makes a healthy heart is what we feed it, *"the mouth speaks out of that which fills the heart."* The Bible calls it "treasure building." Whatever you put into your heart is exactly what will come out. It all depends on what kind of treasure you deposit into your heart.

You can deposit good treasure or evil, depending on what you let in. This is why Proverbs tells us to watch over our hearts! Set a sentry over it that allows only good treasure to be deposited!

> *"Finally, brethren, whatever is true, whatever is honorable, whatever is right, whatever is pure, whatever is lovely, whatever is of good repute, if there is any excellence and if anything worthy of praise, let your mind dwell on these things" (Philip. 4:8).*

Your Thoughts and Your Heart

The thoughts of our minds are important because they form the treasure that eventually makes its way into our hearts. If our treasure is good, we will also be good, but if our treasure is evil, we will be the same. It all depends on what kind of treasure you allow into your heart.

If you allow fearful thoughts to enter your heart, you will develop a fearful heart. You can develop a hardened heart, a callused heart, a shallow heart, or a broken heart. It all depends on what you allow to enter.

You have heard people say, "Boy, that really got my goat." Or maybe you've heard someone say, "That affected me so deeply," or, "I just can't shake it." Those are phrases that indicate whatever was seen or heard was allowed into that person's heart, the very seat of their affections. As a result, the very source of their perspective was altered by it.

I like the way The Message translation paraphrases Proverbs 4:23, *"Keep vigilant watch over your heart; that's where life starts."*

For wisdom and truth will enter the very center of your being, filling your life with joy.

(Pr. 2:10 LB)

We are responsible to keep vigilant watch over what we allow into our hearts. Just because a thought comes into our *mind* does not mean it has permission to drop into our *hearts*. In our minds is where we judge those thoughts as to whether or not they are fit to enter our hearts. If they are not, don't you dare allow them entrance! It will cause bad treasure to build. This is how people get "broken hearts" or "fearful hearts." It is not so much dictated by circumstances or what others have said or done. It is determined by how much of that we have allowed to enter and touch our hearts.

"Above all else, guard your heart, for it affects everything you do," says the New Living Testament. Set a sentry over the lid of your heart, and don't open it indiscriminately. That is what will not only affect your heart, but also everything else in your life!

Evaluate Your Sentry

Be sure that the sentry, whose responsibility it is to watch over your heart, is faithful! Be sure he is trained to lift the lid only for those things that make for the building of good treasures!

Otherwise you'll let in poisons and toxins, robbers and thieves into your control room. That will affect everything about you! If what comes into your thoughts are not of the Lord, don't you dare open the lid to your heart. Judge the thought as unfit for your attention and flush it! We do that with other wasteful things (that I won't mention), so why not for wasteful thoughts?

A Lesson from Jail

While I was in Bible College, I would visit the local county jail from time to time. No, not to be admitted but to speak at the chapel services. This jail was one of the most modern in the state. It was a "keyless" system. The doors were not manually operated, but were opened and closed by an electronic system.

I approached the door on my way to the chapel when a voice over a small loudspeaker began: "May I see your identification, please?"

A bit startled by this faceless voice, I took out my driver's license and held it up. A camera recorded it and the voice continued, "What is your purpose here?"

"I am here to speak at the chapel," I answered, still bewildered.

Just then the door opened. I started to enter when I remembered that I had no idea where the chapel was.

"With good vision you not only see with your eyes but with your heart."

—Zig Ziglar

"Excuse me. Could you tell me how to get to the chapel?"

"Sure," the voice replied. "Just follow the opening doors and I'll lead you there."

Now I had never been directed like that before, but feeling adventurous, I proceeded down the cement corridor. Before long, a door opened to my left, and complying with the faceless instructor, I took a left turn and entered yet another hallway. Half way down this corridor, an elevator door opened. Still figuring an electronic tour guide was leading me, I entered. To my surprise, I found that there were no buttons to push! Blank stainless steel walls greeted me as the elevator doors closed in front of me. The elevator began to ascend.

"Star Trek!" I said to myself. "This is very strange."

The elevator came to a stop, the doors silently slipped into their side pockets, and there I was in the chapel. We had a wonderful time. And when it was over, I asked one of the guards if I could see the control room where my faceless tour guide was housed.

I followed him down several long corridors that led to a small, fully enclosed room with several television monitors. It was surrounded by bullet-proof glass. A few men were monitoring every doorway and every room, and at their discretion, they would allow a person in or out.

I was intrigued by the strength of this new technology, but also quickly saw its vulnerability. I thought to myself, "If the wrong person got into this control room, it could wreak havoc on this whole place. He could control everything!"

Our Hearts: The Control Room of Our Lives

Our hearts are like a control room.

For years, I pushed all the levers and made all the decisions the way I thought they should be made. I tried to handle my life on my own. When that didn't work, I tried the world's way. Things went from bad to worse and everything was negatively affected. When we run our lives according to the world's standards, we begin to live worldly lifestyles.

When I realized my whole life was being adversely affected, I "finally came to my senses" as we find in the story of the prodigal son (Luke 15:17). I opened the door of my heart to Jesus Christ and asked Him to come into the control room of my heart. He began His "house-cleaning" and started changing everything about me.

That is a choice each of us must decide upon. You see, God is a Gentleman, and He will never force Himself on anyone. Instead He knocks and extends the same invitation He gave to me. He offers *"that Christ may dwell in your hearts through faith"* (Eph. 3:17). It will be the most eternal decision you will ever make, and He is available just for the asking.

When He enters, let Him have the controls. He isn't invited in to watch you move the levers and press the buttons. You can't ask Him into your heart so He can give you good luck or simply bless your efforts. He enters to take over!

Meet the Mender of Broken Hearts

Some may still say, "I know now to watch over my heart with all diligence, but the damage has already been done. What do I do if I've already let these thoughts enter? What if others' words have already pierced my confidence and broken my heart?"

Please remember that Jesus came for people just like you! In fact, that was His assignment when the Father sent Him to bring redemption to fallen man:

> *"The Spirit of the Lord God is upon me, because the Lord has anointed me to bring good news to the afflicted;* He has sent me to bind up the brokenhearted." *(Is. 61:1, emphasis mine).*

Jesus can heal your broken heart. That's what He came to do. Ask Him. No one can heal hearts like Jesus can. There's an old rhyme that goes like this:

"Saying 'Yes!' to Jesus: The most eternal decision you'll ever make."
—Wayne Cordeiro

"Humpty Dumpty sat on a wall, Humpty Dumpty had a great fall. All the king's horses and all the king's men, couldn't put Humpty Dumpty together again."

And I would add...

"But the King could. So the King Himself came down from heaven's throne and found all the Humpty Dumpties. Then with the care and compassion that only the King could have, He began to put them together again."

And He is still doing that today. You see, it was for all the broken lives, broken hearts, and broken people that He died on Calvary.

You may think there are certain things you'll never be able to forget. Or maybe you know things that are beyond forgiveness.

When you come to just such an impossible impasse, can I encourage you with one cure-all? He's the only cure-all that really does cure all: Jesus. Only Jesus can heal all things because He paid the price, of His own blood, to cover every sin, every hurt, and even every thought. He offers us the power of His love free for the taking, paid at a dear cost, to cover our most valuable things: our eternity, our hearts and our minds.

Allow Jesus to mend your broken heart. Begin by replacing any broken thoughts with His Word. Then excavate any harmful memories, replacing them with His promises.

And when you begin to accept the amazing grace He has offered, you will begin to see yourself in a whole new light. You will define your life the way He has defined it, and according to His Word. As you allow Him to take you from glory to glory, you will begin to see your thoughts change, your heart become strong, and your life be transformed.

When that begins to happen you will have the most wondrous background music to your life. And if you listen very closely it will sound like the most beautiful, symphonic soundtrack you'll ever experience!

CHAPTER SIX

Practice, Practice, Practice!

"But solid food is for the mature, who because of practice have their senses trained to discern good and evil." (Hebrews 5:14)

Like learning any sport or musical instrument, the more you practice developing an attitude of excellence, the more proficient you'll become at it. Learning to develop a good attitude is no different. It doesn't happen by accident. It needs to be intentional and deliberate, nothing less. It may seem awkward at first, but keep practicing! I remember when I first went to Bible College, I went down one of the hallowed halls and found a huddled group of students congregating in a small circle. I was shy in those days, believe it or not. I was very shy. Being from Hawaii and of a different ethnicity, I was a bit self-conscious, so I was just going to keep walking.

"God is less concerned with what you are doing and more concerned with what you are becoming."

—Wayne Cordeiro

Just then, I remember hearing the Lord speak quietly to my heart. He seemed to say, "Stop and introduce yourself to these students."

All of what I am about to tell you happened within a few nanoseconds, but it left a lifelong impression on me. God doesn't need to use English vocabulary when He speaks. In one atomic moment, He can deposit reams of instruction directly into your heart that will leave your life absolutely transformed.

Instead of changing, I decided to argue with God. "No, that's not me, Lord. You know that's not me. I'm sort of to myself. I'll just pass by these students. They probably don't want me barging into their conversation anyway."

Then I remember the Lord saying, "Do you want to remain what you are today and be that way the rest of your life, or do you want to become what I want you to be? The choice is yours. Right now, you're at a crossroads in your life."

I sensed this urgency and I knew that this was a moment that called for my best response. How often we miss these crossroads of life and our futures are adversely affected because of it. I knew I had to choose and believe I could change.

Taking an immediate detour, I headed right into the middle of the crowd and introduced myself. "Hi! My name is Wayne Cordeiro. I'm from Hawaii. I'm a freshman here at the college. How are you?"

To my surprise, they were gracious and welcoming. I remember their acceptance and their love. Even till this day, a few of those students from that original group are still some of my best friends.

Practice Until it Becomes Comfortable

Ask any backyard athlete that went on to be coached. Many of them had to change the way they held a baseball bat, or shot a basketball, or swung a golf club.

When I first played racquetball, it was against an old cement wall in high school. A group of us picked up some old, dilapidated racquets and started to play. We didn't care too much about form. We just wanted to have fun.

As time went on, I became a bit more serious about the game, so I entered a few tournaments. As much as I played, however, I could never advance beyond a certain level. One day, between matches, an instructor took me aside. He was one of the most renowned racquetball players and instructors on the circuit, so I welcomed his suggestions.

"What you commit yourself to become, determines what you are."

—Tony Campolo

"Wayne, you have some natural talent at this game, but you'll never advance if you don't change your grip. Your form is incorrect."

Well, I'd never heard that before. I asked him if he'd give me a few lessons. However, because we were in the middle of a tournament, we had to schedule the lessons for the following week. Then I asked him what I might be working on until we could get some lessons in.

"Your main problem impeding your progress is the way you're holding the racquet," he said. "Here, let me show you how to hold it properly so you can continue to advance and improve."

He changed the way I had been holding onto the grip for the last ten years! This new grip felt so awkward I almost immediately dismissed it as useless. Sensing my uneasiness, he quickly added: "Even though this may seem uncomfortable, keep practicing until it becomes comfortable. And I guarantee, it will. So stay with it!"

Due to my respect for this instructor and his reputation, I changed my grip and went back to the tournament. I was soundly beaten in all of the following games! Even with my best efforts, I couldn't control the ball. I was sure this new grip was some sabotage effort by an opposing player who put this instructor up to this heinous deed.

The following week, we got together for some lessons and I told him about the new grip. "It's too awkward!" I complained. "What's wrong with my old grip?"

"You can use the old grip, but you'll never advance," he repeated. "If you want to play with the first graders and elderly, that grip will work just fine," he chided. "But if you want to play with the big boys, you can't be holding your racquet that way." That was enough to motivate me. I changed my grip!

But still it felt uncomfortable. He took me through some exercises I would do each day. Over a period of a month, the new grip became as comfortable as the old one. Then I began to advance and improve again.

Act It Before You Feel It

Here's one very practical way to begin.

Have you ever seen a person with a wonderfully contagious attitude? When they enter a room, the atmosphere changes. These people can light up any room. It's not a sham or a put on, it's just something about them that's special. Listen to them talk on the phone. Watch the grace with which they deal with problem people. Observe the way they stand, the posture with which they sit; the way they will slightly lean forward when they are listening to you, nodding in agreement. Watch them. There's something different about their physiology. They sit straighter, they stand taller, and their smiles are genuine.

One of the practice steps in developing an attitude that attracts success begins by changing your physical posture. That's right! You will have a tendency to feel the way you act.

Try slumping your shoulders and hanging your head for a few minutes. Talk like someone really depressed would talk. It won't be long before you'll feel awfully depressed!

Or put a smirk on your face like someone with a really bad attitude would wear. Cock your hip and cross your arms. Look for problems like someone with a bad attitude would. I guarantee that before long, you'll be sporting a genuine, "Grade A," *bad* attitude!

On the other hand, think of a person who has a wonderful attitude! Sit how this person would sit. Speak up like a person with a wonderful disposition would speak. Respond with gentle yet affirming nods when someone is speaking to you, just like a person with a great attitude would when someone speaks with them. I assure you, it won't be long before you'll develop a wonderful attitude!

Even though it may feel a bit awkward to you at first, don't slump back into the old grip you've been using for the past ten years! Stay with it.

Keep practicing until it becomes comfortable!

The Metamorphosis

"My children, with whom I am again in labor until Christ is formed in you." (Gal. 4:19).

The word "formed" in this particular verse is the Greek word, *metamorphon*. Here Paul is talking about the struggle that takes place until there is a metamorphosis in each

If you are without discipline, you are without power."

–Wayne Cordeiro

of us. The old vanishes and the new emerges. It is the picture of a caterpillar *forming* into a butterfly. It is that process where that beautiful creature which is on the inside finally makes its way to the outside!

Paul knew the potential of those Christians in Galatia to whom he was writing. Even though they knew how to live, the knowledge inside their heads hadn't surfaced into their behavior and lifestyle. That was still in its *formation* stages, and Paul had been living in painful anticipation until that which was known would become seen!

Picture a beginning tennis player. He's read all the magazines, watched the videos, and even studied the best plays. He's focused on the smooth delivery of the serve. The ball is tossed gently into the air at a precise height, the tennis racquet is brought over the player's perfectly arched back, and then the smooth explosion rifles the ball into the receiver's court.

Ace!

He's catalogued the perfect tennis form frame-for-frame in his mind. He can mentally visualize this artistic routine, but his actual demonstration of that is far from graceful! He throws the furry sphere higher than expected. The mistimed toss causes him to grunt in crude effort as he shoves the racquet towards the dropping ball. He pushes it awkwardly toward the opposite end of the court, only to have it snagged by the net.

However, with adequate coaching and consistent practice, that graceful *form* begins to emerge. Little by little, we begin to see glimpses of a great tennis player inside! Then as the days go by and the coaching continues, there begins a *metamorphosis* where the inner becomes the outer! His routine becomes increasingly more graceful. What he once only imagined he now is experiencing due to practice. What was once abnormal is now natural and comfortable.

When we see a player like that, in tennis terms, we call that "great form." That is the same word used in Galatians to express to each of us how much the Lord desires for each of us. *"My children, with whom I am again in labor until Christ is formed in you" (Gal. 4:19)*. God's best is in each of us. He created us that way, but what's inside will need time to make its way into our form. That requires practice, but with a little determination and consistency, people will soon be calling you "Ace."

One of the best ways to practice is found in Galatians 5:22-23. Called the *"fruit of the Spirit,"* this section enumerates character qualities the Holy Spirit is in the process of building within us. Underline each character quality you find:

> *"But the fruit of the Spirit is love, joy, peace, patience, kindness, goodness, faithfulness, gentleness, and self-control." (Gal. 5:22-23).*

Each character quality is something the Spirit is trying to produce within us. This tells me that one of the best ways to cooperate with His working is to practice being loving, being joyful, keeping a heart of peace, and so forth. He is faithful to bear these fruits in our lives as we are faithful to practice them.

Rate yourself on each of the following items. Which ones do you need to "practice"? (The areas you would most need to practice would be those that are "least" practiced now.) On a scale of one to ten (with one being "least" and ten being "best"), read each definition and then evaluate what areas you need to prioritize for practice.

	Least									Best
Love	1	2	3	4	5	6	7	8	9	10
Joy	1	2	3	4	5	6	7	8	9	10
Peace	1	2	3	4	5	6	7	8	9	10
Patience	1	2	3	4	5	6	7	8	9	10
Kindness	1	2	3	4	5	6	7	8	9	10
Goodness	1	2	3	4	5	6	7	8	9	10
Faithfulness	1	2	3	4	5	6	7	8	9	10
Gentleness	1	2	3	4	5	6	7	8	9	10
Self-control	1	2	3	4	5	6	7	8	9	10

Love

Am I consistently committed to God's very best in each person's life? Do I treat them as God would?

Joy

Do I trust the fact that God is in control of every situation regardless of how it looks to me? Do I take my joy from knowing this or do I tend to draw my contentment from situations and circumstances?

Peace

Do I bring a calming effect or do I stir up people's feathers? Am I a reconciler or an instigator, a person who fixes the blame or fixes the problem?

Patience

Do I give people room to fail and then help them look for the lessons of life that can be extracted from that failure? Or do I keep score?

Kindness

Am I kind? When working with people under my supervision or care, do I appeal to them kindly or do I have a tendency to order them around? How am I with my own family?

Goodness

Is the core of my heart good? Do I want the success of others or just myself regardless of what happens to others?

Faithfulness

Am I loyal? Can I keep confidences or do I have the tendency to share private information about others? Am I a faithful spouse or do I emotionally court other relationships?

Gentleness

How do I deal with others' failures? Especially if it affects me? Am I more concerned about my welfare or theirs?

Self-control

Do I control my thoughts or do they stray? Am I able to discipline my emotional and sexual desires?

Practice

Take the time to practice these character qualities God is wanting to build in you and express through you. The more you practice these things, the more fruitful you'll be in your attitude, business, ministry, and family. So *practice, practice, practice*!

CHAPTER SEVEN

Never Give Up!

"Nevah, Nevah, Nevah Give Up!"
—Winston Churchill

Let's all agree on one thing: each of us will have the dubious honor of being recipients of life's setbacks. We will all experience speed bumps in life. Suffering is inevitable, misery is an option. Suffering will change you, but not necessarily for the better. You have to *choose* to change for the better.

You can let setbacks become stumbling blocks or steppingstones. They can make you bitter or better. The choice is yours. Remember, life is made up of 10 percent what happens to you and 90 percent how you respond to what happens to you.

One of my favorite scriptures that has given me renewed hope throughout the years has been Proverbs 24:16. It reads, *"For a righteous man falls seven times, and rises again, but the wicked stumble in time of calamity."*

I like that. You see, failure is not when you fall down. It is when you refuse to get up again! Some get knocked down and although they stand up, you can tell they've remained down on the inside.

Pull your spirit up again! Set your sights back on God's purposes for you. The game's not over. You can do so much more! He is able even when you are not!

David stumbled, but he got back up, and God used him to become Israel's greatest king. Jacob stumbled but got back up and became the father of the twelve tribes of Israel. Paul the apostle attempted to annihilate the Christians, but God took hold of his life and used him to take the Gospel to the Gentiles. Peter denied the Lord in His time of greatest need. Yet he got back up, shook off the shame, and God used him mightily to spread the Message of Life to the known world.

The Game's Not Over Yet

In the 1929 Rose Bowl, when Georgia Tech played California, a player by the name of Roy Reagels learned a valuable lesson in the game of life.

Towards the end of the first half, Reagels retrieved a fumble from the Georgia Tech team. He got jostled around in the fight for possession, but finally managed to tuck the ball firmly under his arm and began toward the goal line.

Only one problem ... *he was headed for the wrong goal line!*

Benny Lum, one of his own teammates, took off in hot pursuit of wrong-way Reagels. He finally caught up with Roy and tackled him on their own three-yard line. The next play ended with the California team being tackled in their own end zone for a safety. Those points would become the margin by which they would ultimately lose the game.

At halftime, the team gathered in the locker room. No one said a word. Everyone felt the remorse of the first half, a tragedy that was seen by thousands and thousands of spectators.

The two-minute warning was given, and Coach Nibbs Price finally said, "Okay. The same ones that came out in the first half will start the second." The players headed for the field, all except Roy Reagels. He sat on the bench with his face buried in his hands.

"God did not create you to live life on the sidelines, but to win the game!"

—Dale Galloway

"You heard me Roy," said Coach Price. "I said the same team that came out of the first half will start the second. And that includes you!"

"I can't go out there ever again, Coach. I can't face my teammates. I've let you down, shamed our team, and embarrassed our school. I can't go out there."

Coach Price straightened him up, looked him in the eyes and said, "The game's only half over, Reagels. Get out there and make something of yourself. The game's only half over!"

The Georgia Tech players said they'd never seen anyone play as determined and as intensely as Reagels did the second half of the 1929 Rose Bowl game.

When I recall that story, I think to myself, "Wow. What a great coach that Nibbs Price was!" But then again when I think of our Lord and the way He believes in each of us, I think, "What a great Lord we serve!"

Each of us has stumbled, yet God is not done with us. Granted, there will be a few glitches on the graph of our life, yet He prods us back into the game. He believes in us! You see, the game's not over yet!

The Issue is Love, not Performance

Peter was like that. In the Garden of Gethsemane where Jesus was arrested, Peter fled. Then when Jesus was being tried, Peter denied him not once but three times. Soon after, Jesus was crucified and buried.

I'll bet Peter blamed himself for Jesus' death. I can just hear him, "If only I would have stopped Judas, all this wouldn't have happened. Great leader I am! I can't even stand up to a servant girl asking me if I was a disciple. What a failure!"

In John 21, the whole story changes. Peter felt so disqualified from ministry he traded in his shepherd's staff for a fishing pole and headed back for the lake. Although he knew God had called him to ministry, his recent failures drove him away from that calling.

Jesus stood on the edge of the lake after being resurrected and called to the disciples. When Peter recognized it was the Lord, he left the others behind and swam to the shore. There he sat face to face with the one he had so rudely failed.

I've stood at the spot on the northern shore of Galilee where this meeting took place. There's a plaque depicting this event. I remember being overwhelmed with emotion as a few of us stood there recalling the meeting between Jesus and Peter.

I guess I felt overwhelmed because I so often feel like I've failed, too. Peter's denial seems small compared to the times when I have turned my back on the Lord. How many times I have denied Him, refused to identify with Him, and instead blended in with the crowd.

Yet I can hear Him speak to our hearts just as He addressed Peter: "*...When they had finished breakfast, Jesus said to Simon Peter, 'Simon, son of John, do you love Me more than these?' He said to Him, 'Yes, Lord; You know that I love You.' He said to him, 'Tend My lambs.' He said to him again a second time, 'Simon, son of John, do you love Me?' He said to Him, 'Yes, Lord; You know that I love You.' He said to him, 'Shepherd My sheep.' He said to him the third time, 'Simon, son of John, do you love Me?' Peter was grieved because He said to him the third time, `Do you love Me?' And he said to Him, 'Lord, You know all things; You know that I love You.' Jesus said to him, 'Tend My sheep.'*'" (Jn. 21:15-17)

I am always amazed at the answers of the Lord. If it were me confronting Peter, I would have yelled at him. "You creep! Why did you leave me in a lurch like that? Great friend you are!" I would have confronted his poor performance.

But Jesus didn't confront his performance. He confronted his heart: "Peter, do you love Me?"

"Yes, Lord. I do love You."

"Good. Then get back in the game. It's not over yet!"

The prerequisite for restoration is not performance. It is love. Love will always be God's highest test. Don't put the magnifying glass on your failure. Put it on love, and it will help you see things the way Jesus does. That's always the best way to look at things anyway!

Staying the Course

> *"He will not be disheartened or crushed until He has established justice in the earth." (Is. 42:4).*

One of the most powerful ingredients to developing "staying power," or the ability to get back into the game and stay there, is stubbornness. That's right. You can be stubborn in a right way. I guess you could call it endurance, but I like to call it stubbornness.

Of course you can be stubborn in the wrong way, too. It could be termed "stiff-necked" or "obstinate." But that's not what I am talking about.

Stubborn obedience to a call helps me get through the gauntlet of critics and the nagging memories of past mistakes. I know God has called me to represent Him during my stay on this earth. (He has called you to do the same!) Then, come what may, I must finish the course. I must run the race with endurance-stubborn endurance, mind you-until He takes me home to be with Him forever.

I guess we're in pretty good company because it was prophesied of Jesus in Isaiah that He'd stay the course, too, no matter what came His way. He had made a choice. *He would not be disheartened or crushed until His assignment was through!* He made a choice, and I get to do the same.

We will have many opportunities to bail out along the way. There will be plenty of reasons to resign. I've experienced many! No one ever needs to look far for a reason to get divorced or to leave a home church. There will always be plenty of justification to have an affair. There will always be plenty of sorrows to drown in beer at the local bar.

What will give you longevity is not the absence of stress or trials. Look at Jesus' life. His was riddled with problems. People trying to betray Him, demon possessed people trying to grab onto Him, sick people lining up to touch Him, and Pharisees constantly testing Him. Yet He refused to be disheartened or crushed!

Make the same choice to stay the course. Sure, there may be many course corrections along the way. Maybe even a few deviations from the original flight plan, *but stay the course!*

The Shortest Speech Never to be Forgotten

Sir Winston Churchill was once asked to address his alma mater in a commencement speech. He had become quite a legend by this time due to his courage and confidence during the war.

The auditorium was overflowing with graduating students, parents, dignitaries and guests. He arrived with his classic top hat and coat, stogie, and cane. After an introduction including a long litany of his accomplishments, he slowly made his way to the podium.

Looking over the students, an intensity came over his countenance. He leaned forward and gave the shortest speech those students ever received.

With a tone that was a mixture of warrior and diplomat, he said, "Nevah, nevah, nevah give up!" Taking a deep breath, he repeated with a greater volume, *"Nevah! Nevah! Nevah give up!"* He turned, put on his top hat and coat, took up his cane, picked up his stogie, and left.

We'll all be faced with battles, and when the battles are over, the critics will begin. But nevah give up! You'll want to, no doubt. But the only way the devil can defeat you is if you give him the permission to do so. Don't you do it! The game's not over until God says it is!

The following is a poem written by Kent Keith. It is so appropriate!

ANYWAY

People are unreasonable,
illogical, self-centered.
Love them ANYWAY.
If you do good, people will accuse you
of selfish, ulterior motives.
Do good ANYWAY.
If you are successful, you'll win
false friends and make true enemies.
Succeed ANYWAY.
Honesty and kindness may
make you vulnerable.
Be honest and kind ANYWAY.
The good you do today
may very well be forgotten tomorrow.
But do good ANYWAY.
The biggest people with the
biggest ideas can get shot down
by the smallest people
with the smallest minds.
But think big ANYWAY.

Give the world the best you got.
You may very well get kicked
in the teeth for it.
But give the world the best you got ...
ANYWAY.

CHAPTER EIGHT

Finish Well!

"So teach us to number our days that we may present to Thee a heart of wisdom." (Psalm 90:12)

We have only one life to live for Jesus on this earth, and it will soon be over.

As I grow older, I am increasingly amazed how quickly time passes. It's like the rewinding of a videotape: the closer it gets to home, the faster it goes! So it is with each of us.

As you read this book, as still as it may seem to you right now, you are actually traveling at over 66,000 miles per hour! That's right. That's how fast the earth is orbiting around the sun. Faster than the spin cycle on your washing machine! A few more spins, and we'll be gone.

Don't live a squandered life.

Let's say someone came to you and deposited $86,400 into your account every morning. Wouldn't that be just heavenly! Only one catch: you have to spend it wisely or invest the total amount every day. Any squandering of the money would not be acceptable, the amount would be lost. Nothing could be carried over, anything left in the account will be lost after midnight. Of

Teach us to number our days aright, that we might gain a heart of wisdom.

(Ps. 90:12)

course another $86,400 will be deposited the following morning.

If that were the case, what would you do? You bet! You'd be sure to spend all of it, and it would be spent or invested wisely!

Well, you do have that each day. Only it is not measured in dollars and cents. It is measured in time. Yes, you have 86,400 seconds every day to invest. How you use it is up to you. You can squander it and lose its benefit or you can invest it wisely and be rewarded.

Since we have only one life to give, let's live it well! Your attitude will be the difference between existing and living! It will be what separates a futile life from a fruitful one!

Your Two Most Valuable Decisions

Let me pause at this juncture to ask you again to evaluate the two most important decisions in your life. Your most important decision will be your decision to follow Jesus Christ. That decision will affect your eternity. Your choice to open your heart to Him will be the most eternal decision you will ever make. If you have not done that, don't hesitate for another moment! There is no greater choice than to choose Him to be Lord in your life. It doesn't matter how many possessions you have, how much money you've made, or how much power you've accumulated.

Jesus reminds us in Mark 8:36, *"And how do you benefit if you gain the whole world but lose your own soul in the process?"* (NLT).

Now, as a Christian, let me reveal your second most important decision in life. While your first is your decision to follow Christ, your second will be the *attitude* with which you will follow Christ! The first decision will determine how *eternal* your life will be. The second will determine how *effective* your life will be!

Just because you may be a Christian does not guarantee fruitfulness. How often I have met Christians with poor attitudes that have affected their relationships, family, ministry, and their possibilities for success. This need not be so! Everyone can develop an attitude that attracts success.

Seize the Day!

In the motion picture, "Dead Poet's Society," Robin Williams plays the part of a 1960's iconoclastic English literature teacher named John Keating. Mr. Keating teaches in a buttoned-down, straight-laced, all boys prep school. In his attempt to find new ways to get the boys to learn what would normally be a boring subject, he becomes quite a maverick in his teaching style. This was exampled on the first day of class when he stands behind his desk, and in animated, feverish urgency, implores the boys to follow him outside.

"What would you do if you knew you could not fail?"

—Robert Schuller

He runs out of the classroom and down the corridor to an outdoor rose garden. There the boys gather around him in playful curiosity. With excitement in his voice, he recites a poem:

> *"Gather ye rosebuds while ye may,*
> *Oh the time is yet a flying.*
> *For the flowers ye gather today,*
> *Tomorrow will be dying."*

Turning to the boys, he begins his instruction: "This was originally penned in Latin, and the writer used a phrase to communicate urgency. The phrase is '*carpe diem.*' Do any of you know what '*carpe diem*' means?"

One boy shot his hand in the air, "Seize the day?"

"Yes!" John Keating replies. "And why do you think he used that phrase?"

Another boy takes a shot, "Because he was in some kind of a hurry to write it?"

Imitating the sound of a buzzer, the teacher corrects him, "No, my dear lad. It's because he knew we must seize the moments before us because tomorrow, you'll all be food for the worms!"

"Come!" he calls back as he darted off toward another building.

He gathered the boys around a glass trophy case containing dusty trophies, old memorabilia, and some black and white photographs of former alumni.

"Do you see anything similar in those pictures?" he queried. "Look closely. What do you see?"

His search for an answer is returned only by blank stares, so he continued, "Look closely at them! They're all standing in neat rows. They had the same haircuts as you have. They had the same uniforms as you have. They all had the same dreams and the same hopes and the same aspirations as you have!" He paused to let it sink in, then continued.

"And do you know where each one is right now? That's right. They're all food for the worms! Six feet under!" The boys drew back as if they had come upon some ghastly discovery. Seeing that they were ready for the final lesson, he continued, "But if you'll listen closely, you can hear them whispering their legacy to you. Listen!"

The boys craned their necks back toward the black and white 8 x 10's. Then, as if representing the souls of these past alumni, he whispered in a hoarse voice, intoned with a sense of deep urgency, "*Carpe diem!* Seize the day. Make your lives extraordinary!"

Jesus said it this way, *"You're here to be light, bringing out the God-colors in the world. God is not a secret to be kept. We're going public with this, as public as a city on a hill"* (Mt. 5:14 The Message).

Carpe diem! Seize the day today to bring out the God-colors in your world. Within you lies the Holy Spirit infused through your being by the breath of God. Don't keep it a secret. Begin to live your God-given call by shining your light through your life. You don't have to be a world famous evangelist to shine. Just start by shining your light to those around you every day. And the beacon through which your light will shine to those around you? Your extraordinary attitude.

"Start by shining your light to those around you every day. And the beacon through which your light will shine to those around you? Your extraordinary attitude."

—Wayne Cordeiro

Four Keys to Building an Extraordinary Attitude

Each of us can live extraordinary lives with attitudes of excellence, but it must be diligently cultivated. Let's take a look at four keys to living an extraordinary life.

1. Aim for the Right Target

What are you shooting at in life? What is your goal? If you had only one thing that would drive your life, what would it be?

In the movie, "City Slickers," three sophisticated businessmen decide that their idea of a man's vacation would be herding cattle for a few weeks. Their foreman was a man by the name of Curly, a lone ranging, wizened cowboy, the last of a dying breed.

One day as they're poking along the range, one of the city-slick businessmen and Curly begin to talk about life.

"...[A] Cowboy leads a different kind of life," intones the crusty Curly. "When there *were* cowboys. They're a dying breed. Still means something to me, though. In a couple of days, we'll move this herd across the river, drive them through the valley. Ahhh," he laughs softly, "there's nothing like bringing in the herd."

"You see, now that's great," chirps up the less-rustic businessman. "Your life makes sense to you."

Curly laughs heartily, and the businessman becomes more confused than ever. At this point the worldly wise Curly cuts to the core of this middle-aged businessman's trip. "You all come out here about the same age. Same problems. Spend fifty weeks a year getting knots in your rope-then you think two weeks up here will untie them for you. None of you get it."

The two men fall silent, thinking about the weight of these words.

Curly continues, "Do you know what the secret of life is?"

"No, what?"

Curly raises his weathered hand and seems to point skyward. "This."

"Your finger?"

Still pointing, Curly says, "One thing. Just one thing. You stick to that."

"That's great, but what's the one thing?" prods the eager businessman, seemingly asking for us all.

"That's what you've got to figure out."

If you had just one thing undergirding your life, what would that be? What would you choose to focus on, making it your first priority and your ultimate goal?

Take a look at the list below and decide:

- Money
- Fame
- Prestige
- Power
- Notoriety
- Financial
- Independence/Security
- Being the Best
- Family
- Peace
- Jesus
- Success in Business
- Adequate Retirement
- Sports/Recreation

For many years my choice was "Jesus." But for some reason, without realizing it, He had slipped. I had unknowingly been vacillating for a few years. I was driven more by the fear that I would not have enough retirement, and it skewed my perspective on life. I struggled with periodic pangs of anxiety and I'd be distracted with making just the right investments for my future, constantly watching the stock market fluctuate.

Finally, I revisited my list. It wasn't until I resolved what my true goal in life was that my perspective returned. When my perspective was firmly in place, so was my heart for what God had called me to do.

It all depends on what you are shooting for. When we aim at the wrong target, life itself becomes elusive. Be sure that you are aiming at the right target. Keep your perspective clearly focused on that target, and always double-check to make sure that it's the right target.

"Attempt something so impossible that unless God is in it, it is doomed to failure."

—John Haggai

Take some time out right now, stop rowing through life so frantically, and check to see if you are still headed in the right direction!

What's your one thing?

A Not So Obvious Goal

The Special Olympics is a wonderful organization that encourages children and adults with special learning needs or physical handicaps to compete in athletic events. It is an extremely exhilarating occasion where a parent or guest will have the opportunity to be surprised by the most unpretentious and authentic expressions of life.

It happened in one of the sprints. Young children between the ages of eight and twelve had gathered at the starting line. Some were in wheelchairs, some were in braces, and all were filled with anticipation! The parents and relatives packed the stands, each cheering their own child on with an exuberance that would make the zeal at an NFL championship game pale in comparison.

The race began with the starter's pistol firing into the air. They were off! There were children with crutches, others in wheelchairs and some laboring to control each limb. Those with Down's syndrome ran alongside those with braces. Obvious to all the onlookers was the extra effort of each child. It touched the heart of everyone present.

"You can have everything in life that you want if you simply help enough other people get what they want."

—Zig Ziglar

What brought meaning to the whole event was a child in a wheelchair. She had turned her chair around, moving in reverse with her little feet motoring along to give her more speed. She lost her direction and began to veer off course toward the side. It wasn't long before she ended up against the wall of the grandstands.

Unable to free herself from this predicament, she began to call out for help. A handicapped boy and another with Down's syndrome heard her pleas. They backtracked to where she was, turned her chair around, and began pushing her toward the finish. Amidst the shouts of jubilation and victory, the little retrieval group came across the finish line together.

Their objective was not necessarily to be the one to finish first. You see, they thought their goal was to see that *everyone* made it across the line, and that required the help of every child involved.

What has God asked you to do with your life? Can you name a few of your non-negotiables? If you were to write one paragraph and called it your "Personal Mission Statement," how would it read? You see, if you're not sure about your life's assignment, then how will you know which opportunities to accept and which ones to reject?

In the fabled story of "Alice in Wonderland," Alice loses her way. In the distance, she saw a regal procession being led by the Queen of Hearts. Each soldier resembled a singular playing card as if they were pulled from a deck, given life, and were now marching in military fashion down the road.

"...if you're not sure about your life's assignment, then how will you know which opportunities to accept and which ones to reject?"

—Wayne Cordeiro

Alice, frantic to find her way, stopped the entourage. "Do you know which way I'm to go?" Alice begged.

"It all depends on where it is you really want to end up," answered the Queen. "Well, to tell you the truth, I'm not sure," Alice replied.

The Queen looked quizzically at her and responded, "Then it really doesn't matter what direction you go in, does it?"

If you don't know where you're going, any road will take you there.

Feeling the diffused edges of my life, I sat down and hammered out what I felt was God's direction and assignment for my life and existence. Upon this statement would hang all the activities of my ministry. It would help me to decide what I would say "yes" to and what I would say "no" to. It would act as an internal homing device. It was the race that was set before me. Here is that statement:

> Personal Mission Statement
> Wayne Cordeiro
>
> To model and communicate biblical truths in such a way as to inspire character, equip leaders, heighten the awareness of Jesus Christ, and effectively evangelize those whom God is drawing to Himself.

Where is your road taking you? Do you know where you want to end up? Can you name a few of your non-negotiables? If you do know these things then you're well on your way to success. If you don't, then take a few moments, or even a few days, to pound out your personal mission statement.

Answer the life-changing question, ***"What has God asked you to do with your life?"***

An attitude that attracts success begins with knowing which opportunities to accept and which to reject. And in this way you will begin to develop not just an existence, but a life that is answering God's call every single day.

Remember, first aim for that right target. What are you aiming for? What is your goal? That will determine the race you run.

2. Run the Right Race

> *"Therefore, since we have so great a cloud of witnesses surrounding us, let us also lay aside every encumbrance, and the sin which so easily entangles us, and let us run with endurance* ***the race that is set before us.****" (Heb. 12:1, emphasis mine).*

There is a race God sets before each and every one of us. You cannot run someone else's race, you can only run your own. If you run the wrong race, you'll end up at the wrong finish line.

It happened during an Olympic marathon many years ago. The final stretch of the race brought the runners back into the stadium so those in the grandstands could view the finish. The contestants would run the track for a final lap before crossing the tape.

The first to re-enter was a young man in his twenties. By the time he began the final lap, however, his body was so depleted and exhausted he staggered in delirium. Entering the stadium, he started his run to the right, circling the track in a counterclockwise direction.

"Knowing where you're going is all you need to get there."

—Carl Frederick

He stopped, seemingly confused. His eyes were glazed and his body slumped. He turned and retraced his steps and circled the track in the opposite direction. Stumbling and faltering, he made his way toward the tape. You could feel the sympathy surge from the cheering fans who urged him to turn back. But in his delirium, they sounded like a muffled cacophony of noise. Finally he found the tape, staggered through it and collapsed. A few minutes later the other runners entered the stadium and the race concluded. When the results were announced, to everyone's dismay, the first runner had been disqualified. In his confused state, he had circled the stadium in the wrong direction thus causing him to run to the wrong finish line.

Sometimes, we as Christians can live discontented lives because we are going after the wrong finish lines. We put in Herculean effort but we aren't investing in what God wants us to invest in. Instead, we have our own predetermined desires and we use God to help us get where we want to go. We use God like a genie in a magic lamp. We try to rub God the right way so He will answer our prayers the way we want them answered. We don't wait for counsel so we ask God to bless what we're doing rather than to help us do what He's blessing. Our prayer may resemble this: "God, I want You to help me to find my fulfillment in life. Then I will be content."

Train yourself to be godly. For physical training is of some value, but godliness has value for all things, holding promise for both the present life and the life to come.

(1 Tim. 4:7b-8)

Instead, pray this prayer. It will change your perspective. It will trim your lamp. It will help you to stay on track and finish well!

> *"Lord, here is my life. Use my life for Your purposes and Your desires. Lord, come live Your life through me. Whatever I have, whatever skills I may possess, whatever my abilities and capabilities, finances or treasures, Lord, I lay them at Your feet. How can You use them? You instruct me so I can be a faithful steward and use my life for Your purposes. Whether I have much or little, I will be content because I know You are using my life for Your purposes. Come, Lord, live Your life through me."*

Instead of *telling God* what you'll do for Him, ***ask*** Him to do His work through you! Instead of *telling God* how you plan to live for Him, ***ask*** Him what His plans are for your life. By doing this you will tap into His power to fulfill His plans His way! There's no greater satisfaction then when you are experiencing the surge of His life through your soul!

> *"'For I know the plans that I have for you,' declares the Lord, 'plans for welfare and not for calamity to give you a future and a hope.'" (Jeremiah 29:11)*

3. Understand What Satisfies Your Soul

> *"Therefore, do not worry saying, what shall we eat or what shall we drink or what shall we wear, for indeed your heavenly father knows that you have need of all these things. But, seek first the Kingdom of God and His righteousness and all these things will be given to you as well" (Mt. 6:31-33).*

Jesus gives us the secret of contentment. It cannot be acquired directly. Rather, contentment is a by-product of a life that is focused on the right things. Truly content people are the ones whose aim in life is something much bigger than attaining mere contentment alone.

If your sole aim is to acquire possessions and money in order to be comfortable and content, then contentment will be as elusive as a butterfly.

A few years ago, the whole world had its eyes on an American billionaire who wanted to fly the fastest plane in the world. So he designed, built, and piloted the world's fastest airplane. He wanted to have boats and condos and live in exotic places. So, he bought them. He amassed such a great fortune that he had two United States presidents at his bidding. He believed he could gain contentment by having more affairs and sexual endeavors, more expeditions, explorations, and excursions. So, that is what he did.

Let's fast forward the tape to the end of his life. His hair is long and unkempt, his beard disheveled, and his arms are filled with the puncture marks of a drug addict frantically attempting to jab contentment into his veins. His fingernails were long and unruly, resembling pale yellow corkscrews. Bedridden, he would sit in a drug-induced trance peering at life through his dark, sunken eye sockets and emaciated body. He had missed life itself.

He purchased a large hotel and lived there in self-imposed solitary confinement. He was a man desperately searching for contentment but never finding it. He died in a very lonely pit of despair trapped in a hollow skeletal shell. I am sure you will recognize his name: Howard Hughes. He lived his whole life hoping to find contentment, but ended up empty-handed. He traded his soul for possessions and lost it all in the final stretch.

"A wise fellow should have money in his head, but not in his heart."

—Jonathan Swift

Read what Jesus said in a parable about a rich man's foolish words in Luke 12:19-21,

> *"...I will say to my soul, 'Soul, you have many goods laid up for many years to come; take your ease, eat, drink and be merry.' But God said to him, 'You fool! This very night your soul is required of you; and now who will own what you have prepared?' So is the man who lays up treasure for himself, and is not rich toward God."*

I recall when the famous humorist and television show host Johnny Carson retired. He made millions of dollars from his late night talk show. With all his fortune, his candor and colorful jokes, you'd think he'd be one of the happiest people around. Instead, in an interview, one of his relatives reported, "Johnny is one of the saddest people I know. He's someone who's always looking for a good time, but never finding it."

"How happy you are depends to a very large degree on your relationships with other people."

—Zig Ziglar

Jesus reminds us in Luke 12:15, *"Beware, and be on your guard against every form of greed; for not even when one has an abundance does his life consist of his possessions."*

Understand what truly satisfies you; what satisfies your soul. Otherwise, you'll never be able to develop an attitude of true contentment. You'll be always looking for a good time but never finding it. Instead, choose to learn the vital concept of knowing what satisfies your soul.

4. Contentment: An Inside Job

"I have learned to be content in whatever circumstances I am. I know how to get along with humble means, and I also know how to live in prosperity; in any and every circumstance I have learned the secret of being filled and going hungry, both of having abundance and suffering need" (Philip. 4:11-12).

Paul did not live a cushioned, aristocratic life, yet he had developed a world class attitude that carried him through every storm. Paul knew what it meant to have little because he had been hungry. Paul had been abandoned. He had been stoned, shipwrecked, whipped, beaten, and left for dead. Paul was someone who had been mocked at, lied about, ridiculed and slandered. When he wrote these words about contentment, he was writing them from prison. He was facing the fact that within a few years, he would be tortured to death. How in the world was he able to maintain a godly attitude under his circumstances? How could he possibly say he knew what it meant to be content?

Because his aim in life was much bigger than contentment itself. Paul's aim was not to attain a lifestyle of convenience and comfort. Paul's aim was to know God and to serve Him with all his heart. His goals were accurate. His desire was that his life would somehow, in some way, be used to bring God's purposes to pass. He sought first the Kingdom of God by using his skills, his influence, and whatever he could so the Lord could use them. Then, contentment flooded his life, and his attitude turned his prison cell into the place where nearly half the New Testament would be penned!

Contentment is vital in developing an extraordinary attitude. It's the final and critical key in your process. Each of these four keys are simple but eternally priceless. Remember, start off right by aiming for the right target, the one God has for you as you *"run your particular race to win"* (Heb. 12:1). The next step is to *just do it*! Run the right race. The last two fit hand in hand: understand what satisfies your soul and do so by learning contentment. With these keys you'll be well on your way to developing an extraordinary attitude for an extraordinary life!

CHAPTER NINE

Back to the Source

"Have this attitude in yourselves which was also in Christ Jesus." (Philip. 2:5)

During a class on American history, some second graders were asked, "Can you name the foreigner who was a big help to the American colonists during the Revolutionary War?" Billy quickly raised his hand, and when called upon, confidently answered, "God!"

The bottom line of developing an attitude that attracts success is not simply found in positive thinking. Don't get me wrong. There is nothing wrong with positive thinking! When you consider the alternative, negative thinking is no option!

"Positive thinking is the hope that you can move mountains. Positive believing is the same hope but with a reason for believing you can do it."

—Zig Ziglar

However, it must go far beyond that. E. Stanley Jones once said, "Anything less than God will let you down." Jesus said in John 15:5, *"Apart from Me you can do nothing."*

We desperately need His help, and if we ask Him, He will never turn us down. *"Ask and you shall receive, seek and you shall find, knock and the door shall be opened unto you"* (Mt. 7:7).

God is the only One I know who can change the human heart. Government can't, money won't, and ideal circumstances don't.

Only God can. Without Him, our efforts would be futile at best.

"Unless the Lord builds the house, the laborers labor in vain." (Ps. 127:1).

Developing a world class attitude takes decisiveness, commitment, perseverance, and a willingness to be effective at this thing called life. Your attitude, in essence, is the expression of your faith and the display of your character. Without God's help and direct, moment-by-moment involvement, none of this would be possible.

"Your attitude, in essence, is the expression of your faith and the display of your character."

—Wayne Cordeiro

It is not simply the result of "positive thinking." It is the result of Jesus Christ's working in your life and your cooperation with His instructions. Here are two ways in which the Lord will help you to develop an attitude like His:

1. The Bible

The Bible is the greatest book on life ever written. It is the best book on leadership, business, family, marriage, and everything else that pertains to life. When God's Word fills our minds, we can't help but develop a better attitude! Especially when His instructions and counsel begins to find its way into our conversation, relationships, and habits. Then our attitudes will be transformed.

We will have two teachers in life: the teacher of *wisdom* or the teacher of *consequences*. Both are tremendous teachers, and you will learn from both. There is a price to be paid to enroll in each class. However the price that must be paid to the teacher of consequences may cost you everything you have. For some it has cost them years, others have paid with their futures, and for some it has cost them their families. You will learn from consequences, though the program may take you years and years. For some, it has taken them a lifetime to learn what they should have long ago. "Consequences" can be an effective teacher, but a cruel taskmaster, nevertheless.

Your word is a lamp to my feet and a light for my path.

(Psalm 119:105)

Wisdom on the other hand, comes from lessons learned vicariously through other's consequences. You can learn through other's experiences without having to go through the pain yourself.

There is a pain in wisdom as well, because wisdom requires you to develop something called *discipline*. When you would rather get angry than be patient, discipline is painful! When you want to tell someone off but you know it would be wiser to let it go, it is painful!

There are two pains in life: the pain of discipline and the pain of consequences. The pain of discipline will cost you pennies, whereas the pain of regret can cost you millions.

Making Wisdom a Sport

"Doing wickedness is like sport to a fool, and so is wisdom to a man of understanding" (Pr. 10:23).

One "homespun" principle I follow is derived from Proverbs 10:23. It depicts a fool who makes a sport out of doing wicked things. Interestingly enough, the writer then compares that fool to a man of understanding. Instead of making a sport of wickedness, the man of understanding makes a sport of wisdom!

He who gets wisdom loves his own soul; he who keeps understanding will find good.

(Pr. 19:8)

What an interesting idea: to make a sport of doing what would be wise. I love sports and can get fairly competitive, so this was speaking my language! The Bible was giving me permission to train for and inaugurate a new sport, the sport of wisdom.

Here's how it works in my life. When I come to an impasse or a problem, the game begins. Others may bail out saying, "It can't be done." They say it's "impossible." I hear that all the time, but in actuality, they have only succeeded in disqualifying themselves. Instead, let the games begin!

I try to figure out what the wisest thing to do in this situation would be. Here's the great thing about this sport: you can get help, counsel, or advice from anyone you wish! It's not cheating! You can recruit thinkers, problem solvers, and you can read any books you like to get fresh answers and new ways of looking at the problem. The only rule is that you must do it the biblical way. Your goal is to solve the problem in the wisest way possible.

So I ask God for wisdom. James 1:5 says, *"But if any of you lacks wisdom, let him ask of God, who gives to all men generously and without reproach, and it will be given to him."* Pretty good deal!

Solomon asked God for wisdom and it so pleased God that He gave Solomon much, much more than what he had asked! Read these words in 1 Kings as Solomon asked God to help him with wisdom so he could rule the people of Israel well:

> *"And it was pleasing in the sight of the Lord that Solomon had asked this thing. And God said to him, 'Because you have asked this thing and have not asked for yourself long life, nor have asked riches for yourself, nor have you asked for the life of your enemies, but have asked for yourself discernment to understand justice, behold, I have done according to your words. Behold, I have given you a wise and discerning heart, so that there has been no one like you before you, nor shall one like you arise after you. And I have also given you what you have not asked,*

"Want to be wise? Listen to your Father. Want to be foolish? Don't. Life is simple."

—Wayne Cordeiro

> *both riches and honor, so that there will not be any among the kings like you all your days'"* (1 Kings 3:10-13).

This has helped me more than you'll ever realize. I'm still a beginner at this sport, but with a little more practice, I hope to keep advancing.

The Source of "Wisdom Training"

> *"All Scripture is inspired by God and profitable for teaching, for reproof, for correction, for training in righteousness; that the man of God may be adequate, equipped for every good work"* (2 Tim. 3:16-17).

Getting wisdom can come from many different sources. We can learn a great deal through experiencing everything firsthand and feeling the pang of consequences, but that may not be the best way. Yet even though experiencing consequences can be a good teacher, wisdom is far more desirable. How?

What if there was a way we could gather the top 400 leaders of all time and have them become our teachers and mentors. Wouldn't that be fabulous? But even a year with them wouldn't be enough. Then, what if we took the accounts of their lives and recorded them in a book? Better yet, what if their experiences were edited so only the most profound and critical lessons were recorded, ones that would be most useful to us. How much would you pay for a book like this? I'd be willing to pay thousands of dollars for this treasure!

Well, God already compiled one of these for you. It is called the Bible. In it are the best of the best and God had their lives edited so we can read about their experiences and the consequences of their actions. Instead of us having to go through what they did, through wisdom's instruction, we deposit the gems of what they learned into our hearts and our lives are transformed!

David said in the book of Psalms, *"I have more insight than all my teachers for I meditate on your statutes"* (Ps. 119:99). In other words, the instructions of God's Word will give you wisdom beyond your years! His Word will be the ageless mentor to help each of us be *"conformed to the image of His Son"* (Ro. 8:29).

Develop a consistency of reading the Bible on a daily basis. Each day you will receive another gem God will tuck into your heart. As He hides His Word into your life, you'll begin to see a day-to-day transformation, an ever-increasing likeness to Jesus.

The mistakes you commonly would make in the past will begin to become more infrequent as the Holy Spirit guides your words and actions. *"Thy Word have I treasured in my heart that I may not sin against Thee"* (Ps. 119:11). The Bible is one of God's best tools in helping you to develop an attitude that attracts success!

2. Prayer

> *"And He came out and proceeded as was His custom to the Mount of Olives; and the disciples also followed Him" (Lk. 22:39, emphasis mine).*

Prayer is one of the more elusive exercises in a Christian's life. It's like watering a plant. You may not see immediate results, but if neglected, the consequences can be disastrous. It must be a habit, a daily habit.

When you take the time to pray through your upcoming decisions and plans, you are beginning to learn how to think deeply in the presence of God. He helps you by His Spirit and gives you wisdom and insight. Keep a journal near you when you are praying to jot down instruction and understanding the Lord reveals to you. I often fill my own journal with page after page of what God reveals to me about my attitude, my faith, my perspective, or my behavior.

Rejoice always; pray without ceasing; in everything give thanks; for this is God's will for you in Christ Jesus.

(1 Thes. 5:16-18)

Remember, however, that prayer is not simply another venue to complain before God. Often we misuse prayer and simply use

God to try and get our own agenda accomplished. Our attitude in prayer is important! Listen to what Paul says in Colossians: *"Devote yourselves to prayer, keeping alert in it with an attitude of thanksgiving."* (Col. 4:2). He reminds us to keep an attitude of thanksgiving!

Billy Graham once gave a short illustration of the results prayer should have on us. He was watching a ship pull into the dock. Thick ropes were fastened to the dock and the huge engines of the ship began to whir. Then he noticed something intriguing. As the ropes drew taut, he noticed the dock wasn't drawn to the ship, but the ship was drawn to the dock!

Prayer should be exactly like that. When we pray, we don't pull God down to our level in order for Him to accomplish what we've got assigned for Him to do. Instead, prayer draws us firstly near to God in order that we receive His strength to do His bidding! How often we forget God doesn't exist for our purposes. We exist for His!

It is in prayer that God begins to reveal simple but key truths that help us to see things from a whole new vantagepoint. When you pray aright, you can't help but have your attitude changed!

> *"And in the same way—by our faith—the Holy Spirit helps us with our daily problems and in our praying. For we don't even*

> *know what we should pray for nor how to pray as we should, but the Holy Spirit prays for us..." (Ro. 8:26).*

Now You Get To Choose!

> *"I call heaven and earth to witness against you today, that I have set before you life and death, the blessing and the curse. So choose life in order that you may live, you and your descendants." (Deut. 30:19).*

Developing an attitude that attracts success is a choice each of us must make. Let me remind you again: the most important decision you'll ever make in life is your decision to follow Jesus Christ. This decision will determine the *eternity of your life.*

The second most important decision you'll make will be the *attitude* with which you will follow Jesus Christ. This decision will determine the *quality of your life!*

Moses told God's people they had a choice, either life or death. He even revealed the outcome of their decision that one will bring a curse and the other will result in life!

Two Prisoners

The story is told of two prisoners lying on their bunk beds one evening. The prisoner on the top bunk was staring out the window of his cell into the night sky. The stars spread out in a splendid array of constellations, with an occasional shooting star making the evening sky a spectacular display of divine fireworks.

Turning to his cellmate in the bunk below, he said, "Hey, wake up! Look at the stars! They're beautiful. Look!"

"Aw, leave me alone," his cellmate grunted.

"Come on. Just look. The stars tonight are the brightest I've ever seen!"

Laboriously and with great effort, his cellmate turned over in his bunk to look at the night sky. After a short glance, he gruffly replied, "I don't see no stars. All I see are the bars."

One saw the stars and the other saw the bars. It all depends on your attitude doesn't it? Contentment is an inside job. You will either be a master or a victim of your attitude.

See the Stars

So too, God sets before you the decision of serving Him either with a great attitude or with a poor one. Choose a good one that you might experience life! Yes, life for you as well as your descendants! It takes training, discipline, and a desire to develop your perspective to see what's good. Choose, because both will be present, the stars as well as the bars. Look for the stars, and you'll reach them! Look for the bars, and they'll surely imprison you.

Look for the stars. They're out tonight. Then follow them. They just may lead you to a bright future!

You're only one attitude away from a fantastic life!

About the Author

Pastor Wayne Cordeiro, a dynamic and motivational communicator of God's Word, is Senior Pastor of New Hope Christian Fellowship O'ahu—one of the fastest growing churches in the nation. New Hope O'ahu grew to over 6,000 regular attendees during its first 4 years in addition to planting 17 New Hope churches throughout the Pacific Rim and Montana. Pastor Wayne is a published songwriter with five albums and has authored several books including *Gems Along the Way* and *Doing Church as a Team*. He and his wife Anna have been married since 1974 and have three children—Amy, Aaron, and Abigail.

Other Resources from Wayne Cordeiro

Bible Training
Pacific Rim Bible Institute

Books
Doing Church as a Team (in English, French, Korean, Japanese, & Spanish)
Gems Along the Way (in English and Japanese)

Conferences
Doing Church as a Team Conference

Leadership
Hawaii Leadership Practicum (One-week Pastoral Shadowing Program)

Music
Lately I've Been Learning
With All Our Hearts (New Hope O'ahu Praise & Worship Band)

Teaching
Sermon Series
Small Group Tool Kits

Visit Pastor Wayne at New Hope Christian Fellowship O‘ahu’s website at www.newhope-hawaii.org

For a free resource catalog please contact:
New Hope Christian Fellowship O‘ahu
ATTN: Resources Dept.
290 Sand Island Access Rd.
Honolulu, HI 96819
Phone: (808) 842.4242 ext. 604
Fax: (808) 842.4241